MW00817723

DEDICATION

I dedicate these books to the courageous men and women, most of whom will remain forever anonymous, who, through the five million year course of human development, have brought the Man/Woman Game this far, and left it, finally, up to us.

the MAN WOMAN book

THE TRANSFORMATION OF LOVE

For further copies of this and other transforming books and tapes, write:

Ron Smothermon
Context Publications
P. O. Box 2909
Rohnert Park, CA 94928

Or call (707) 584-4423

RON SMOTHERMON, M.D.

CONTEXT PUBLICATIONS

ACKNOWLEDGMENTS

I honor the women in my life, beginning with my Mother, who have been kind enough to put up with me, share life with me, and tell me the truth of a woman's experience of a man. God bless women.

I honor the men in my life, beginning with my Father, who, by being men, made me a man, and revealed to me what a man is.

I honor my son Houston who is source of the inspiration with which I am blessed.

FOREWORD

There are two states of being in which God is met: in love, and in near-death. I have met God in near-death, and have had the opportunity, and the choice, to live or die. It was more inviting to die than I can tell you—the peace available in death is beyond description—and my work is not complete. I chose life. Nevertheless, I enjoy the ecstasy of being in the presence of God, and because I am not ready to die, the subject of these books is love—the other state of being in which God is met. I am using life to teach me about love, to be in the presence of God, and I invite you to join me.

In the prevailing philosophy we have created about love, love is two things: rare and special. These books are a radical departure from that prevailing philosophy of love.

Our work is the transformation of love. When it is complete, we, as humankind, will wake up each morning filled with love and compassion for our husband, wife, or lover, for our parents, our children, for our neighbors, for people over the world, many of whom we will never know personally, and even for our relatives—not because of heroic effort on our parts, and not because those people deserve it, and not because we have transformed ourselves into saints, but simply because Absolute Love will be the way it is.

There will be a monument to our work. Our monument will be anonymity—when people know they love each other simply because that is the way it is, we will not be eulogized or remembered for the work we are doing now to bring forth that reality. Our monument will be the absoluteness of love itself, and we will live in that temple for eternity.

TABLE OF CONTENTS

Introduction and Preparation to Read These Books

Origin of These Books 7
Fundamental Definitions 9
Purpose in Reading These Books 11
Leaving Patterns 13
What to Do, and Not Do,
With The Information in These Books 15

Book I: The Man/Woman Relationship

Chapter 1: Definition 21
Chapter 2: The Stakes For Which We Think We Play—
    Feeling Good 25
Chapter 3: The Stakes For Which We Do Play—The Future . 28
Chapter 4: Macho—The Thing in the Driver's Seat 32
Chapter 5: The Feminine Principle—
    What is it and Where is it? 36
Chapter 6: The Individual's Relationship to the Whole 39

Worksheet 42

Book II: Honesty

Chapter 1: Honesty and Dishonesty—the Definition 45
Chapter 2: All Have Sinned 48
Chapter 3: To Be—The Results of Honesty 51

Worksheet 55

Book III: The Realms

Chapter 1: Paradise Lost—Born into a World of Opposites . . 58
Chapter 2: Paradise Regained—The Realm of Absolutes 61
Chapter 3: Reconstructing Reality 65

Worksheet 69

Book IV: Mother—One's Relationship With All Women

Chapter 1: Earliest Beginnings 72
Chapter 2: The Purpose of a Parent 75
Chapter 3: What Is a Woman?—The List 78
Chapter 4: Becoming The List—Being the Definition 80
Chapter 5: Taking it Away—The Result of
              Withdrawing the Acknowledgment of Mother . . . 84
Chapter 6: A System Which Excludes Its Creator 87
Chapter 7: Re-creating Relationship With Mother—
              Who Mother Is, and Isn't 90
Chapter 8: The Acknowledgment of Mother 94

Worksheet 97

Book V: Father—One's Relationship With All Men

Chapter 1: The Brick Wall and The Soft Heart 100
Chapter 2: A Father's Job—To Hold a Vision 103
Chapter 3: The Scapegoat 105
Chapter 4: Creating Who You Are—
              Figuring Out Who You Are Not 107
Chapter 5: The Father List—What Is a Man? 110
Chapter 6: Becoming Authentic With Father and With Men 112
Chapter 7: The Acknowledgment of Father 115

Worksheet 118

Book VI: Personality and Change

Chapter 1: The Answer 121
Chapter 2: Patterns 124
Chapter 3: Surrender 127
Chapter 4: Enlightenment 130

Worksheet 132

Book VII: Telling It Like It Is

Chapter 1: The Club—Domination 135
Chapter 2: The Auxiliary—Mean—
         The Price for Domination 138
Chapter 3: The Potential for Violence—The Real Issue 141
Chapter 4: The Role of Fairy Tales...................... 144
Chapter 5: What Every Man Searches For—
         A Nice Virgin Princess...................... 147
Chapter 6: What Every Woman Searches For—
         A Non-Macho Prince 150

Worksheet 152

Book VIII: Origin of The Man/Woman Relationship

Chapter 1: How Long Is Five Million Years? 155
Chapter 2: The Invention of Agriculture 159
Chapter 3: The Coming of Cities, Technology,
         and Commerce 162
Chapter 4: Prepared for Something Else—
         Hunting and Homemaking................... 164
Chapter 5: The Origins of Domination—Love and Need ... 167
Chapter 6: The Origins of Mean—
         Non-preparation for Technology 170
Chapter 7: A Man's Jealousy—
         Don't Steal My Property, or I'll Kill You 173
Chapter 8: A Woman's Jealousy—
         I've Got to Have One or I'll Die............... 176

Worksheet 178

Book IX: Compassion—So Missing That No-one Noticed

Chapter 1: Compassion—What Is It? Where Is It? 181
Chapter 2: To Forgive a Man............................ 184
Chapter 3: To Forgive a Woman 186

Worksheet 189

Book X: Creating, Maintaining, and Ending Relationships

Chapter 1: The Wheel of Relationship—
           Choosing a Partner While Awake 192
Chapter 2: The Create a Relationship Game.............. 197
Chapter 3: Sex, Power, and Authority—
           Removing the Mystery 199
Chapter 4: Choosing and Being Chosen 202
Chapter 4: Ending Relationship Forms—
           Its Not As Bad As You Think 105
Chapter 5: Loyalty.................................... 208

Worksheet 209

A Salute to the Reader 210

Completion Exercise 211

Where to Go From Here 212

Invitation 213

Answers to Awakeness Exercises 214

Index of Words, Terms, and Phrases 230

INTRODUCTION AND
PREPARATION TO READ THESE BOOKS

Origin of These Books 7
Fundamental Definitions 9
Purpose in Reading These Books 11
Leaving Patterns...................................... 13
What to Do, and Not Do,
With The Information in These Books 15

THE ORIGIN OF THESE BOOKS

In September, 1982 I was asked to present a seminar in a distant city. I asked the Person who had extended the invitation what subject he wanted. He said that he would leave that up to me.

When I asked myself in what area I had that kind of knowledge, I could see several possibilities, and one area stood out as the area in which the evidence of my life clearly demonstrated that I had little knowledge or skill: man/woman. In looking at that, I saw an odd discrepancy: I knew little, and I knew that I knew little, and still I had the thought that I knew it all.

In that realization was a challenge I could not pass up, so I entitled the seminar The Empowering Man/Woman Relationship Training and bravely flew off a couple months later to deliver information I did not possess.

Thus the Man/Woman Training was created through faithful reliance on inspiration in the moment of delivery, and on the inspiration and partnership of the participants. I realized that an inspired training would be worth far more than a smart training, especially for me, the person who most needed this training.

The event was quite successful by most standards, and soon a network of people around the country picked up on the fact that I had delivered a training on man/woman and the invitations to deliver it in other cities poured in. Twenty-five trainings were delivered in 1983, and 1984 saw more growth. The early trainings were not good, by my standards, and the recent trainings have been outstanding, even by my unreasonable standards.

Two factors qualify me to source this material into existence. First, I know that I don't know it all, even though, like all men, I have a thought that I do. Second, I take a life-long stand on the potential of the Man/Woman Relationship.

My training to bring you this material began 20 years ago when God took the man most in need of The Man/Woman Training and over the next 20 years jammed him through a Crash Course. This Crash Course was delivered, and continues to be delivered, by confronting him with all the upsets of the Man/Woman Relationship in his own life experience. The avoidance of these upsets had, as a matter of fact, become my life. I first realized that I was in a training about the time the first Man/Woman Training was delivered in 1982.

The data itself is an evolving body of information which behaves like an organism, growing and mutating each time it is presented. It is committed to making a difference about the Man/Woman Relationship.

The presentation of the Man/Woman Relationship in modern life is that it makes so little difference that no-one has noticed that there is a Man/Woman Relationship, a relationship all men have with all women and all women have with all men, a Relationship from which our individual relationships are derived and in whose boundaries our individual relationships are confined and express themselves.

FUNDAMENTAL DEFINITIONS
OF THE PERSON

To make what I write be a source of power requires that you know five terms which I use often. These terms are: Being, Self, Personality, Instinct, and Mind. These are the five fundamental components of a Person.

When I write the word "you," I am referring to this wholistic Person of five component parts. By "wholistic," I mean that the Self, Personality, Instinct, and Mind all reflect the Being.

These definitions come from Nothing, which is the context from which the Being comes, the context in which the mastery of life appears.

BEING

The Being is the link between this physical plane and a reality which is hidden, of which we glimpse only a few times in this life—those times when we love absolutely.

The Being is the opportunity from which all Persons come. It has the purpose to create, and be the space of creation for, the Self.

The Being is the player in the Game of Life. It creates that which is seen and apprehended, and, not being a "thing," and demonstrating no process, cannot itself be seen or apprehended. Its existence is inferred by the evidence of its creations.

The two expressions of the Being are: (1) original questions about the nature of reality and life, based on Nothing, and (2) the ability to create the Self. That which does these two things is, by definition, the Being.

SELF

The Self is the first expression of the Being. It is the aggregate sum of all the answers to the questions the Being raises about life and the nature of reality. Said another way, the Self is the sum of all promises the Being gives about life, which have the effect of organizing one's experience of life and of reality. It is the background against which life is seen.

The questions raised by the Being span a wide range from, for example, "What is a chair?" to "What is the purpose of life?" The part of the Self that is the answer to the question "What is the purpose of life?" can survive the death of the states listed below, until it is complete, that is, until the purpose of the Being for that life is achieved. This happens when life becomes a strong stand for the answer. Persons whose lives were such stands include Christ, Clair Booth Luce, Martin Luther King, Jr. and Ghandi. I am sure you can name others. We remember those names because their purpose in life is not yet completed, and lives on in us.

The Self has the ability to live in other Selves. In The World, the Person's name comes to represent the Self.

PERSONALITY

The first creation of the Self is the Personality. The Personality is a complex set of behavior patterns the Self uses to act upon the situations of the Game of Life.

The purpose of the Personality is to achieve the Self, that is, to attain the Being's purpose for a life, and to prove the nature of reality to be what the Self claims it to be.

INSTINCT

The Instinct is the body's drives, with its three billion year (the duration of life on earth) history of adaptation to the environment in which the Game of Life is played out. The Instinct's aims are to maintain life by avoiding death and to procreate life. Thus, hunger, thirst, and the desire for sex are the functions of the Instinct; eating, drinking, and sexing are its activities.

MIND

The demands of the Instinct and the demands of the Being, Self, and Personality, are often at odds with each other, as well as with other Persons. The Mind exists as a mechanism to mediate the components of the Person to each other and to other Persons. The Mind functions through judgment, evaluation, explanation, and justification, all of which is used for a singular purpose: to make one's Person right. Feelings and emotions are part of the justifying mechanism of the Mind, and exist to mediate the component parts of the Person. The Mind, together with the the Instinct, is confined to the body, unlike the other components of the Person.

PURPOSE IN READING THESE BOOKS

Here is a secret about life: you always achieve what you intend to achieve. Another way of saying that, in this instance, is that you will achieve from reading these books, exactly what you now, in this moment, take a stand for achieving. I will tell you another secret: it naturally follows that you can achieve anything you are willing to take a stand for achieving.

If you are reading these books as an "interesting" pass-time, you will be very "interested" in what you read here, and you will report to your friends how "interesting" these books are. If you are reading these books to discover that you already knew all that stuff anyway, you will come to the last page, and regardless of what I wrote, your words will be "Hey! I knew that already!" If you are reading these books to be confused, you will wonder what I mean on every page.

I predict this: you are likely to read these books and run your rackets with books, authors, and the Man/Woman Relationship. You will, that is, unless you wake up now, and read while awake rather than while asleep.

If I were reading these books, I would not settle for what I could expect from the experience. I would settle for nothing less than that which I could not expect. When something happens which could not have been predicted by logic, that is called a "miracle." Miracles reorder logic. If I were you, I would settle for nothing less than miracles in my relationship with the opposite sex.

So, if what you want from reading these books is reasonable, I say "So what?" You can have what is reasonable by waiting, reading nothing, and spending no money. Just wait.

To have what is unreasonable, to have the miraculous in your life, requires that you have the purpose of miracles in what you do. Miracles are a function of the Being because it is the Being which defines purpose.

I leave you a space below to make a list of miracles. Give a date to each one, and when you have completed the list make it real and let go of it. By "let go of it" I mean put the list out of your mind, destroy it, do not think of the dates you wrote down, settle back and enjoy these books.

INTENDED MIRACLE	by	INTENDED DATE AND TIME
1.	by	1.
2.	by	2.
3.	by	3.
4.	by	4.
5.	by	5.
6.	by	6.
7.	by	7.
8.	by	8.

Now staple or tape this page shut and literally forget it. If you think about it between now and the time of the intended miracles, there will be no miracles. Later you will notice there are a couple of pages shut together and you will open them to see your list and realize that it all came to pass.

This is the simple technology of releasing the power of the Being to create miracles.

LEAVING PATTERNS

You may think this volume is for entertainment, and in fact you may be entertained as you read parts of it. However, if you read it in the Context of Entertainment, it will not make much difference in your life beyond simple, temporary entertainment. There is a potential for much more here than entertainment.

I give you fair warning: some of the material in these books may disturb you at a deep level. The experience you have in going through the data of these books will parallel, and on some occasions recreate exactly, your experience of being confronted with difficult situations with the opposite sex.

People demonstrate a wide variety of patterns in dealing with that which is uncomfortable for them, so there are not many predictions I can make about how you will want to deal with this data.

There is one exception, however. Almost everyone I know has, as part of his or her bag of behavior patterns in response to uncomfortable situations, this solution: leave.

When it becomes uncomfortable with your boyfriend, girlfriend, husband, wife, lover, or friend, one of the solutions that presents itself is to find the door and leave. This pattern is so automatic, one doesn't have to think about it. You simply find your eyes wandering to the nearest exit, your body stands up and takes you away.

So, one thing I can promise you could happen, as you read these books, is that you could, without thinking, lay it down and "forget" to come back, or "lose" the volume, or "loan" it to someone and never see it again. Leaving Patterns are clever and can exercise their purpose without your conscious cooperation.

In fact, the most damaging thing you can do to yourself when you are disturbed with something is leave it and never complete with it.

Therefore, if you really mean to derive your above-stated purposes in reading these books, you would do well to give a promise to complete a certain amount of it each time you pick it up, then keep it in a place where you cannot lose it. Record on your schedule when you will read again, and repeat this procedure until completion. Do not loan this volume out.

To achieve your intended results, you must read these books in the order in which they were written and complete each exercise.

I leave below a page for you to schedule your reading of each of these ten books. Give a date and time to each book and then write it into your schedule.

Book	Date and Time I Will Read the Data and Complete the Exercises
Book I	
Book II	
Book III	
Book IV	
Book V	
Book VI	
Book VII	
Book VIII	
Book IX	
Book X	

If you did not fill in this list, you are reading these books for entertainment. I wouldn't bother, if I were you.

WHAT TO DO, AND NOT DO, WITH THE INFORMATION IN THESE BOOKS

It could be that you should not read these books. There are severe upsets buried in the Man/Woman Relationship, and therefore in your individual relationship with the other sex. If you read these books consciously, with an intention to create value from them, those upsets will necessarily come up in your own life experience, just as they have in mine over the past 20 years.

There are two ways to deal with upsets. You can use them to invalidate yourself and others, or you can use them as an opportunity for growth. If you know yourself well enough to know that you use upsets to invalidate yourself and others, then do not read these books, for it will not be a valuable experience for you.

I promise you only two things in reading these books. The rest of the results you may want are up to you to create by your own intention. The two results I promise you from a conscious study of these books are acceleration and upset. The events which are already waiting to happen in your relationship with the other sex will happen more rapidly, and as a result, you will be upset. Like being on a roller-coaster, the upset comes with the acceleration.

There is an even greater danger in your reading of these books. The danger is that your reading, that is, the way you read this data—not the way it is written, but the way you read it—will make no difference in your life, in your experience. Even though you experience acceleration, the difference it makes will not penetrate to you.

The real danger in this is that the Condition of Life—that nothing makes a difference anyway—will have been further strengthened. Many people did not pick up this volume because of previous disappointments with books that promised much and delivered little. Unless you lend your power to the reading of these books, that could happen here, also.

I write to empower you, and for that to happen requires that you empower what I write.

When a person reads information, that instrument which is used to read it, the Mind, sees the data through the Filter of Opposites. Our world exists in a Realm called Opposites, where every thing and every idea exists only by virtue of the existence of its opposites.

Place an object in front of you. A cup will do fine. That cup exists as a function of everything else in the universe which we could call "not-that-cup." Except for not-that-cup, that cup does not exist.

Without up, there is no down. Without north, there is no south. In the Realm of Opposites north invalidates or proves south, up invalidates or proves down. Let's hit closer to home: without winners there are no losers, and vice-versa. That notion reeks great devastation upon humankind.

So, when you attempt to learn new information, the Realm of Opposites presents itself as your attempt to believe it or disbelieve it. In the Realm of Opposites you can't be north if you are south; alternatively, there can only be a north if south exists. The value of data is lost when you first begin to consider whether or not you will believe or validate it by invalidating its opposite.

There is another realm from which data can be assimilated, and this realm is almost never experienced spontaneously. It is the Realm of Absolutes. In the Realm of Absolutes, there are no opposites—reality exists as a whole, not as diametric parts—and the issues of belief and disbelief do not appear. In the Realm of Absolutes, it is a matter of being with information, not a matter of arguing with it or agreeing with it.

In the Realm of Absolutes there is absolute value to all information and all experience. For example, you go to a mountain-side to see a sunset, and you can see it through the Realm of Opposites or the Realm of Absolutes. Through the Realm of Opposites you compare it to other sunsets you have seen, and while you are comparing you miss the reality of the sunset before you.

Or you have a date with a new person, and while comparing that person with other people you have been out with, you miss who your date is altogether.

Seen in the Realm of Absolutes the sunset, and the new person, exist in a unique, incomparable beauty of their own.

Few people assimilate data from the Realm of Absolutes. In fact, few people know how to create the Realm of Absolutes in the first place.

Consider this, unless you are a world champion speed reader, these books will take several hours, or days, of your time to read. If you are going to invest that much time, as well as the money you spent for this volume, wouldn't you be wise to read from the Realm of Absolute Value? (By the way, I hope this volume wasn't loaned to you. For you to derive the maximum value from it, you need to have spent your own money for it.) So how does one create The Realm of Absolute Value?

The method is deceptively simple. Understanding it is no problem. The problem is in mustering the courage to use the method, for in creating this Realm you admit the fact of your sole responsibility for your life.

Here is the method:

(1) First give a promise to yourself that you will create great value from reading these books. This promise should be so strong that I could write in ancient Chinese characters and you would receive incredible value from reading them, even if you did not understand a word.

(2) Then be willing to back up your promise with your life, for the rest of your life. In other words, you would live or die to keep your promise to create great value from reading these books, and if you re-read it years from now, your promise will still produce great value for you.

Whether or not you have your relationship with the other sex transformed out of your relationship with these books is up to you, and the method for that transformation, creation of a Context of Absolute Value, is contained in the two steps above.

Some people will swear by these books for the rest of their lives. Others will swear at these books for the rest of their lives. What is the difference?

The difference is that some people will use the steps above to exist in the Realm of Absolute Value as they read this book, and others will read these books from the Realm of Opposites from which, I promise you, nothing matters or makes a difference, even though it is possible to be entertained in that Realm.

You will know when you are in the Realm of Opposites—you will notice that you are believing or disbelieving what you are reading.

The data contained in these books is not to be believed or disbelieved. Be warned: I will throw in some mis-information, and some outright lies, from time to time, just to keep you honest, and to be sure that you do not try to believe or disbelieve what I write.

This data is actually a stand, the fruition of a promise I gave some years ago to cause a transformation of the Man/Woman Relationship. This is a promise you may want to give at the end of these books. In fact, if you don't, you will have missed the point. The most effective way of fulfilling this promise is to offer other people the opportunity to make that promise and take that stand.

For now, simply create a Realm or Context of Absolute Value. If you do, you will know it by presenting yourself, as you read, as a person who can be contributed to.

Most of us, most of the time, cannot be contributed to, because we want it our way, and we want to be right. So, let's get one thing straight. You are right. Now, don't waste time proving it.

BOOK I
THE MAN/WOMAN
RELATIONSHIP

The biggest news of this entire volume about the Man/Woman Relationship is that there is one.

Book I: The Man/Woman Relationship

Chapter 1: Definition 21
Chapter 2: The Stakes For Which We Think We Play—
            Feeling Good 25
Chapter 3: The Stakes For Which We Do Play—The Future . 28
Chapter 4: Macho—The Thing in the Driver's Seat........ 32
Chapter 5: The Feminine Principle—
            What is it and Where is it? 36
Chapter 6: The Individual's Relationship to the Whole 39

Worksheet 42

CHAPTER 1
DEFINITIONS

*Each individual bears the responsibility to derive
an answer to the question "What is the Man/Woman
Relationship?"*

For the experience of these books to make any sense to you
requires that we make a distinction, or definition, about men and
women. It is literally true that no-one has noticed that there is a
Man/Woman Relationship, a common ground from which we all
come in relating to the other sex.

The Man/Woman Relationship is derived out of the entire history
of human experience upon the earth. It comes out of the adapta-
tions to the threats to our survival we have made over the past five,
or more, million years of human development. These
behavior/thought/feeling patterns which have worked to survive
this species through the passage of time contribute a large part of
the Man/Woman Relationship. We are animals, creatures of instinct.

The Man/Woman Relationship is also, and equally, derived from
a spiritual, or thought, source: our individual, arbitrarily chosen
beliefs about the nature of men and women. We are godly, creatures
of spirit and thought.

So, what I am saying is that the Man/Woman Relationship is
derived from two sources. One is from the Instinct, a biochemical,
hormonal, in short animal source, bound in our bodies. The other
is derived from pure thought, a structure of beliefs, a stand we take
about the matter, that is, a spiritual source.

The first, instinctual, source is constant and unchanging, derived
from an unimaginable number of generations of human beings
adapting to the environment, relating to the other sex in such a
way as to cause the survival of both the individual and the species.

The second, spiritual source, in its present form, has been created
much more recently, perhaps in the last few hundred years. This
pure thought source of the Man/Woman Relationship is subject
to change over a period of several life-times. Even within a single

21

life-time we can see some movement.

The instinctual man/woman relationship will not change, regardless of what we think about it, except in a time frame of millions of years. That which requires millions of years to develop requires millions of years to mutate. Don't wait for human nature to change in your own life-time. You will grow old and never have any fun. Furthermore, change is not necessary to a transformation of the Man/Woman Relationship.

So, the Man/Woman Relationship is the common ground from which we all come in relating to the opposite sex. All humankind shares the Instinctual Man/Woman Relationship, and all humankind shares certain basic assumptions of the spiritual Man/Woman Relationship, that relationship which is derived from pure thought, and is a function of all the Selves of the world.

The assertion I am making here is that there is such a common ground. There is a lot of evidence for this assertion which I will be presenting throughout these books. However, at this time, I am not asking you to do anything more than entertain the assertion, not believe it, or disbelieve it, simply entertain it.

If we look at life through the notion that there is a common ground from which we all come in our relationship with the other sex, then what we are interested in is a working answer to the question: "What is this common ground?", that is "What is the Man/Woman Relationship?", as precisely as we can define it.

Our criteria for any such definition should be the mastery it provides in living in a world populated largely by strange aliens: members of the opposite sex.

The entire purpose of these books is to allow you to define a working answer, a set of assertions, to the question "What is the Man/Woman Relationship?" To the degree that you derive a working, not rigid unchanging, answer to this question, consistent with objective and subjective reality, you will have ease in deriving value from these books. My job is to present enough data for you to derive your own working answer.

A good working answer is always open to modification based on reality testing. My working answer to the question "What is the Man/Woman Relationship?" is flexible and open-ended. I am not going to present you with any final answers, for that would not empower you.

You will probably think I believe what I write. That is merely an assumption you make, because *you* try to be right by believing what *you* think. I do not think what I write is The Truth, otherwise I could not write it, and I do not believe it.

I am here to provide useful questions, and open up areas for questions which we assume are closed and unknowable, so much so that perhaps we do not notice those areas existing. Nothing is closed and unknowable, and there is much in life which is unnoticed.

Before we go further, I have a question for you to be with: In the long run, for humankind, which of the following is of greater significance: the relationship between East and West, Democrats and Republicans, North and South, liberals and conservatives, or the relationship between man and woman? Do not answer that question. Simply be with it.

The Awakeness Exercise

After each chapter, there will be a list of questions. Before going on, write down your answers to these questions, then grade yourself by the answers at the end of this collection of books. If you score less than 100%, re-study the chapter before proceeding to the list of insights and declarations. This test is not intended to "grade" you on the "right" answers, rather it is intended for you to see if you read the material while awake or asleep.

1. What is the Man/Woman Relationship?

2. What are the two sources of the Man/Woman Relationship?

3. Which component of the Man/Woman Relationship can change, and which component cannot change?

4. Over what time frame has the Man/Woman Relationship developed to its present form?

5. For our purposes, any definition you derive in answer to the question "What is the Man/Woman Relationship?" will be judged how?

For answers see page 214

CHAPTER 2
THE STAKES FOR WHICH
WE THINK WE PLAY
Feeling Good

Comfort is the reward we seek in playing the Man/Woman Game. Lonliness is the greatest possible loss we can imagine.

In a certain way, life is a game, made up of many other games. The choice to play the game called Life is made when one is born. The rules are simple. To win the Big Game of Life, simply stay alive. You can lose many of the smaller games within the game called Life, and still win Life by staying alive.

Of course, ultimately, we lose the game called Life. And, for the time we are winning, the game usually seems worth it.

Among the smaller games of Life, the largest and most important one is Man/Woman. It includes, and interfaces with, all the other games, including Money, Power, Spirituality—you name it. Most of us define success in the Man/Woman Game in approximately these terms:

> Attainment of a satisfying, and joy-filled, state between oneself and members of the opposite sex.

> (Thus do most of us loose.)

It is an ambitious and exciting game. Ambitious because it is difficult to win, and exciting by virtue of the sexual energy in the Man/Woman Game. This energy is a direct expression of Instinctual life energy. You have it, whether you love it or hate it, even if you have sworn it off, and it is a vast reservoir of power to achieve the Being's purpose for your life. It works this way, however, only when integrated into the whole Person.

Any game you choose to play has stakes. If you approach a gaming table in Las Vegas, you expect risks of loss and possibilities of reward. The Man/Woman Game is no different—there are risks of loss and possibilities of reward. The risk of loss, for most of us, is no more than lonliness. The possibility of reward, for most of us, is no more than satisfying relationships with people of the opposite sex.

These are the stakes for which we think we play. If you win with these stakes, life is nice, people of the opposite sex treat you with love and respect. Your greatest fear, if you should lose, is dying alone, without love, respect, and companionship.

These are big stakes when you look at life from a personal point of view, and almost no-one sees beyond the personal point of view.

The Awakeness Exercise

1. How does one win the Big Game of Life?

2. Which game includes, and interfaces with, almost all the other games in the Big Game of Life?

3. What is a vast reservoir of Life Energy available to you to achieve the Being's purpose for your life?

4. What is required for you to harness and use this energy?

5. What are the stakes for which we think we play in the Man/Woman Game?

For answers see page 214

CHAPTER 3
THE STAKES FOR WHICH WE DO PLAY
The Future

Suppose you find a game for which the stakes are life or death, and you are required to play? Exciting, yes? Now, what if the game is for everyone's life or death, in other words, for the future of human life on earth? And, you are required to play. Very exciting, yes?

Let's say that you like games, and you take a trip to Las Vegas, find a table with a card game, inquire about the stakes and one of the players points to the nickels on the table. You think you can handle those kinds of stakes, that it would be fun to win a pile of nickels, and not the end of the world if you lost a few. So you join the game.

You play all night, and as the new day breaks you see that you lost a lot of nickels. So you cash in to go get some sleep. As you are leaving the table, the dealer tells you that each nickel represents a thousand dollars. You look at the other players expecting a big laugh and they look back at you indicating agreement, that indeed each nickel represents a thousand dollars. You are in shocked disbelief.

As you are led away to see the owner of the casino, who is not a very nice Person under these circumstances, you see your whole life going down the drain.

This is not a likely story, since in Las Vegas the stakes are made plain when you enter a game. However, it is an excellent analogy to the Man/Woman Game, because the actual stakes of the Man/Woman Game are not clear, and they may be much larger than mere comfort and happiness.

The stakes we think we play for are the experiences of comfort, happiness, joy, companionship, etc. If we discovered that these were just nickel stakes, compared to the real stakes, what might the real stakes be?

Let's talk about a possible end to the Life Game for a moment. If humankind is an experiment in the Grand Cosmic Game, is it possible that the experiment called "Humankind" could come to an end? As a matter of fact, it is very possible.

The means to end the Game are already at hand. There are keys and buttons in the world right now, which if turned and pushed, would end the Human Experiment. Many intelligent people are convinced that our specie will be extinct very soon.

Now let's say, just for the sake of discussion, that no-one ever activates the computers, turns the keys, pushes the buttons. Let us say that a madman never gains the authority or ability to do that. Let's say that a terrorist group never gets its sweaty hands on a nuclear device. Let's give ourselves the benefit of the doubt, and say that ultimately all of us will have more sense than to blow the earth away, intentionally. I find this very unlikely, and let's be generous, and say that it will never happen by human intention. Is there any other way the destructive power of nuclear weapons can be released?

Let us look for a moment to the discipline of statistics with its possibilities and probabilities. If there is a potential for something to happen, even if it is not probable, only possible, and if enough time is added to the equation, statistics and common sense say that eventually it will happen. In other words, we are dealing here with what is ordinarily termed an "accident."

Therefore, the existence of nuclear weapons plus enough time equals many flashes of light in which we all disappear, except for a few who perish as a result of radiation over the next several weeks, and the rest who perish in a global, nuclear winter in the following months.

All we need, therefore, to come to The End is the possibility plus enough time, and there is plenty of both. If infinite time is added to a possibility equation, the possibility becomes a certainty.

I live to remove the possibility so that infinite time can be added to the equation without occurrence of nuclear catastrophe. I do not live in the hopes that it will never happen while there is a possibility. I know it will.

Let's back up a bit and look at how such a situation could have developed in the first place. Could it have anything to do with the

Man/Woman Game? To find a working answer, let's think of humanity as a group of people on a bus, the Bus of Life, headed down a road, the Road of History.

As we look backwards, down the road from which we came, we see the incredible suffering in difficult circumstances from which we all came. We can see our ancestors eeking out a hand-to-mouth existence in the most difficult of conditions.

As we look outside the Bus, at the present, we see, on one side of the Bus, starvation—millions of people dying of hunger on a regular on-going basis.

On another part of the Landscape of the Present are mountains of excess food going to waste, more than enough to feed these starving people. There is the capacity to educate those people to feed themselves, which is what those people want, and inside the Bus an argument about what, if anything, to do about it.

On the other side of the Bus we see conventional warfare raging in many parts of the world. And when we peer up the Road of History, into the future, what we all see is a blinding flash of light, the end of life on earth as we know it. It isn't clear how far up the road it is, and all of us, who look, see it.

Inside the Bus we are frantically looking for a solution. Some of us think if we all sit on the right-hand, capitalist side of the Bus, everything will work out. Others of us think if we all sit on the left-hand, socialist/communist, side of the Bus, all will be well. A few are undecided and there is a loud debate about right or left going on inside the Bus.

No-one has noticed that the world exists in the Realm of Opposites, and that the East/West Oppositional Polarity, or something just like it, is inevitable in the Realm of Opposites.

Nor has anyone thought to see who, or what, is driving the Bus straight toward the blinding flash of light.

If we discovered that whatever it is in the driver's seat has something to do with the Man/Woman Game, it might make the stakes we think we play for more like life or death, or in other words the future of the Human Experiment—not how it turns out, which is another issue, but its very existence, whether there will be a future or not.

The Awakeness Exercise

1. Is it possible for the Game of Life to End? If so, how?

2. If we never end the Life Game by intention, is it possible for it to end another way? If so, How?

3. The existence of nuclear weapons plus what equals The End?

4. What is on either side of the Bus of Life?

5. What is down the Road of History if we continue in our present direction?

For answers see page 214

CHAPTER 4
MACHO
The Thing in the Driver's Seat

With rare exceptions, men, not women, are run-
ning the war machines of the world. There is no question
about that. I have a different question: What is running
men?

Let's see what has its hands on the steering wheel of the Bus.
As we look at it, it turns out to be male, not female. In other words,
as we look at what controls the governments of the world, which
have power over nuclear strikes, we see that there are almost no
females to be seen. As we look out over the Congress of the United
States, The Joint Chiefs of Staff of the Armed Services, Politburo
of the Kremlin, the Parliaments of England or India, to name only
a few, the number of women is almost too insignificant to count.
In other words, whatever it is at the steering wheel of this Bus is
definitely male.

Looking closer at the driver's seat we see that it is not individual
men, rather a male characteristic. If a woman is willing to display
this characteristic, she can get her hands on the wheel, also.

It is embodied in the very name of our nuclear policies, which
in the U. S. is termed "Mutual Assured Destruction" or M. A. D.
for short. In other words, if you hit me, I will hit you back so hard,
we will both be destroyed mutually. To every man, or boy-becoming-
a-man, those words have a familiar ring.

In the life of every boy-becoming-a-man, there came a time,
around age 8 to 10 years of age, when he realized that his life was
in danger. The danger was in being destroyed by a bully. Every
boy on the earth faces that possibility, those in India, those in Africa,
those in the U. S., those in Russia, those in England—a universal
human experience of growing up male.

Soon it became a daily experience of fear of death, and every
man alive has in his Mind the name of one or more bullies who
terrorized him. Men who are 40, 50, 60 or more years old still have

those names in Mind and have no difficulty recalling them. If you are reading this, and you are a woman, and doubt what I am telling you, ask any man.

This situation has its origin in the history of development of the species, and we will look closely at that later. (See Book VIII, Chapter 4) For right now, I want you to simply focus on the role fear plays in becoming a man.

If you were small and afraid, and moreover you were asked to learn complex systems such as multiplication tables, spelling of complex words, etc., you might find yourself in a bind. Unable to function and learn, in a fear-paralysis, you would look for a solution. You might give yourself a pep-talk. You might say something to lessen your fears, such as:

1. I am better than that bully. I don't deserve this kind of treatment. If push comes to shove, the adults will see this and save me, or

2. He may be stronger than I am, but I am certainly faster. It would be humiliating, and I could outrun him and get away, or

3. I may not look like it, and I am stronger, I could certainly win a fight if I had to, or

4. If all else fails, I am smarter than that dunce and I could outsmart him and save myself some way or another.

So, now you have a set of four assertions, a pep-talk which, when you give it to yourself, you feel better. So, to function and learn your school lessons, you give yourself this pep-talk over and over, many times each day, because the fear is always with you. You say "I am better, faster, stronger, smarter" over and over, and it works! And, for the next ten years you repeat this to yourself every day of your life until finally you don't think it anymore. You, in fact, become it, and think the rest of your thoughts from it.

When you tell yourself something, like "I am better, faster, stronger, smarter," over and over for years, you eventually stop thinking it and become it. It is a stand you take and, as such, it is a piece of your Self. Every boy takes this stand in becoming a man. We have a name for this set of thoughts, "I am better, faster, stronger, smarter," which all men are, and that name is the "Macho Male Ego," which is nothing more or less than this set of four simple thoughts. We will occasionally abbreviate it the MME.

When it comes to making or evaluating something like nuclear policy, men don't think "We are better, faster, stronger, smarter," or the underlying thought which is "They want to harm us;" men think from those thoughts, plan from those thoughts, and act from those thoughts. Men are so certain that those statements are true, many of us cannot think them consciously.

So, that which is in the driver's seat of the Bus of Life is the Macho Male Ego, a simple set of thoughts: "I am better, faster, stronger, smarter," from which all men think. While the MME is in the driver's seat, M. A. D. is the only nuclear policy possible for the world.

If this is so, where are the women, or more precisely, where is the Feminine Principle, the counter-point to the Macho Male Ego?

The Awakeness Exercise

1. What is running men?

2. What is in charge of the war machines of The World?

3. How can women get their hands on the steering wheel of the Bus of Life under present circumstances?

4. What is the Macho Male Ego?

5. What is the purpose of the MME?

6. In what age range do males develop an MME?

7. Which men do not have an MME?

For answers see page 214

CHAPTER 5
THE FEMININE PRINCIPLE
What is it and where is it?

*If we discovered that women have a quality which
would counter-balance the Macho Male Ego, would it
be worth knowing about?*

Before we look to see where the Feminine Principle is located
in the Bus, let's ask ourselves what it is. I will define it thus: the
ability to find solutions to problems without resorting to violence
or domination by threat of violence.

(Do you think a council of women would have come up with
Mutual Assured Destruction as a solution to the problem of the
existence of nuclear weapons?)

To find the Feminine Principle, we must look all the way to the
back of the Bus where it is sitting in silence. In other words, in
the Bus of Life, the women are in the back. The women who are
closest to the front are gripping and complaining about how the
Bus is being driven, and other women are rearranging seats in the
back of the Bus. The women on the back row are riding in silence,
and there is another group of women riding in the luggage com-
partment. They are not only not heard from, they are not even seen
in public.

Why are women in the back of the Bus? Four factors keep them
there:

(1) the notion that what the individual does, doesn't matter,
(2) fear of men,
(3) fear of losing the chance to ever have a man, and
(4) the derision of men.

We will deal with the notion that what the individual does doesn't
matter in the next chapter.

Regarding fear of men, if you are a man reading these words you
need to know that women feel, in relationship to men, the way
you felt in relationship to the bully when you were 12 years old.

You probably were not beaten up, or if you were it wasn't more often than required to establish dominance. The real pain in the situation was the fear and humiliation of the ever-present possibility of being beaten up. Women constantly experience that fear and humiliation in the presence of men at a subliminal, often conscious, level. That doesn't make sense to most men, and it is true. If you are a man, and you do not believe this, ask any woman.

Every woman has, built into her physiology, located approximately in her solar plexus, the thought "I have got to have a man, or I am going to die." It is a thought built in by untold generations of women for whom, in prehistoric times, and for many in historic times, it was literally true that each woman had to have a man or risk death as a result.

This thought is associated with a sinking feeling like the one boys have when confronted with the bully. This thought and feeling come up for women particularly at night, when alone, without a man.

Please understand the severe ambivalence women have about men. On the one hand women fear men and on the other hand the greater fear is of not having one. If all men knew this simple fact, the Man/Woman Relationship would shift immediately.

The final factor that keeps the Feminine Principle in the back of the Bus of Life is the derision and scorn men have for women who move forward in the Bus to take on more responsibility in life. This too, is an instinctual reaction, on the part of men, and it comes from ancient circumstances when such a move by a woman would have threatened the survival of the family or tribe.

The Awakeness Exercise

1. What is the Feminine Principle?

2. In the Bus of Life, where is the Feminine Principle?

3. Why do women fear men at a subliminal or conscious level?

4. Every women has, built into her physiology, a thought, located approximately in her solar plexus. What is it?

5. Where does this thought come from?

6. Under what circumstances does this thought come up most often?

7. What factors keep the Feminine Principle in the back of the Bus of Life?

For answers see page 215

CHAPTER 6
THE INDIVIDUAL'S RELATIONSHIP
TO THE WHOLE

All Beings exist in a matrix. When one Being shifts,
the matrix itself shifts and thus do all Beings shift, in
time. The ultimate secret of life is the reality of death.
Those who know this secret strive to shift the matrix
and leave their marks upon the earth.

If you take the time to examine what you assume about making a difference in life, you will realize that the fog you must penetrate in order to see any possibility of making a difference is a pervasive thought: "I don't make a difference anyhow, no-one does, so why try?" In other words, what we think from in life is that the individual doesn't make any difference.

We come to this conclusion and take this stand because our criteria for determining whether we make any difference or not have nothing to do with whether or not we actually make a difference. That false criteria is credit, recognition, and acknowledgment. Did we get recognition, acknowledgment, and credit for what we did? Do people agree that we made a difference?

If not, according to these criteria, then no difference was made. According to these criteria, one must be praised in the newspapers or the evening news to make any difference in life. Viewed through these criteria, almost no-one makes a difference.

Now, let's look at reality. Is it true that recognition, acknowledgment, and credit are necessary to make a difference? When the question is clearly stated, the answer is a certain "No, of course not!" Many people have made a large difference in your life and received little or no recognition for it.

You could list those people now, and it would be a long list. If you look at the list, you will soon realize that those people contributed to you in a way that you could, and have, passed the contribution on, in a way that the recipients have passed it on, and so forth. There are people living who have made contributions to humanity of gigantic proportions, whose names we will never know. I give you a space here to list six such people out of your own life:

1.   4.

2.   5.

3.   6.

How many of these people were praised, and received credit for the contribution they made to humanity? How many made the evening news for it?

Life, then, is an ever-shifting matrix, wherein when one intersection (individual) in the matrix shifts, the entire matrix shifts. When you take a stand to live a transformed life, all lives experience a shift, and few of those people know who caused it.

What you do, and don't do, makes a large difference in the matrix of life. Most of us are waiting to be moved, and not exercising our ability to move and contribute. The difference made by remaining passive is measured in terms of what didn't happen, rather than in terms of what did happen. This is a powerful way of making a profound difference.

The beauty in knowing this is that it sets life aright to know that your life matters. The difference between a life lived in purpose, and knowledge of making a difference, and a life lived not in that knowledge, is the difference between day and night.

To the subject at hand, the manner in which you experience and conduct your relationship with the opposite sex has a profound effect on the Man/Woman Relationship, the common ground from which we all come in relating to the opposite sex.

All of us know, intellectually, that life will end someday. A few of us know this in more than an intellectual way. The finiteness of life, when not denied, leads one to live life with the purpose to contribute, to make a difference by having lived. If you knew this ultimate secret of life, the reality of death, could you continue to hold your relationship with the other sex in a small context? Could you continue to treat people of the other sex in the way you now treat them?

The Awakeness Exercise

1. To know that we make any difference in life, what is the fog we must penetrate?

2. What are the false criteria we use to find out if we make a difference or not?

3. What happens when one intersection is a matrix shifts?

4. What is the ultimate secret of life?

For answers see page 215

At the end of each section there will be a page like this one. If you are reading these books for a difference to be made in your relationship to the opposite sex, it is necessary to use these pages thoroughly. This is called the "Worksheet."

Here is an outline of the data in this section, for your review:

Book I: The Man/Woman Relationship

Chapter 1: Definition 21
Chapter 2: The Stakes For Which We Think We Play—
        Feeling Good 25
Chapter 3: The Stakes For Which We Do Play—The Future . 28
Chapter 4: Macho—The Thing in the Driver's Seat......... 32
Chapter 5: The Feminine Principle—
        What is it and Where is it? 36
Chapter 6: The Individual's Relationship to the Whole 39

Insights into my own life which I have created as a result of reading Book I:

1.

2.

3.

4.

5.

Actions I plan to take based on these insights, including the date by which time each one will be completed.

1.

2.

3.

4.

5.

BOOK II
HONESTY

*Bound in the quality of one's honesty and
integrity is the quality of one's life, itself.*

Book II: Honesty

Chapter 1: Honesty and Dishonesty—the Definition 45
Chapter 2: All Have Sinned 48
Chapter 3: To Be—The Results of Honesty 51

Worksheet 55

CHAPTER 1
HONESTY
The Definition

*To manifest adult honesty requires an adult defini-
tion. Most of us operate from a child's definition.*

As children we are told to be honest, and we are told that what
that means is to not lie, cheat, or steal. Rarely is a child told why
not to lie, cheat, or steal, and when told, the reasons given insult
the child's intelligence. Furthermore, honesty is presented to
children as a passive quality—actions one does not take. We do
not teach honesty as an active quality—something one does as an
act of honesty, or otherwise one is not honest. The result is a world
full of passive liars—people who will not tell the truth when it is
time to tell the truth.

So, in discussing the properties of honesty, I will have an adult
conversation with you, recognizing that you may never have had
an adult conversation about honesty. You were probably never told
anything convincing about honesty by your parents, and if you
were, that was only their experience or concept, not yours.

If you want to develop solid reasons to stay honest, you will have
to do a very unpleasant experiment called Being Dishonest, and
dispassionately observe the results. Once the results become clear
to you, you can rationally choose to be honest or not. It isn't a pretty
way to become honest, and it is ever so lasting.

Although I rarely write from the "story" aspect of my life, the
abstractions about which I write *are* derived from my own life experience. I simply leave me out so there can be room for you. I
speak to you abstractly from my own experience of being honest
and dishonest. What I tell you is true for me. I have paid the price
to know my principles.

There is much more to being honest than not telling lies. Honesty
is also an action one takes. It is an act of telling the truth. Dishonesty,
on the other hand, can be an act or a non-act. Telling untrue information is dishonest, and so is withholding the truth when it is

time to tell it. But, this goes deeper than information.

Honesty requires truthful representation of your experience, as well as the information at hand, expressed for no other purpose than the expression itself. There are situations when it is time to express the truth of how you feel, and if you withhold that, you are a liar, and will pay a liar's price. Also, if you use telling the truth of your experience as a weapon to punish others, you are lying, and will pay a liar's price.

There is another realm of honesty which is harder to define. It is the realm of *being* honest, which goes beyond doing honest. Being honest is represented by telling the truth to the best of your knowledge and experience, at your own responsibility.

If you are being honest for someone else, or if you are being honest for something you believe in, or if you are being honest for a reward, or to avoid punishment, or to reward or punish others, then you are not *being* honest, although you may be *doing* honest.

The Awakeness Exercise

1. Are children taught that honesty is a passive or active quality? That is, are children taught that honesty is something you do, don't do, or both?

2. What are the two components of honesty?

3. How does one do honest?

4. How does one be honest?

5. How does one do dishonest?

6. How does one be dishonest? (You will have to think for this answer. It is implied, and not expressly stated in the text.)

For answers see page 215

CHAPTER 2
ALL HAVE SINNED

If you say you are not a liar, you have proved
yourself to be a liar.

Complete honesty is a difficult state to attain. You can approximate it, or perhaps even create it for a few moments. If you do, you will forever refer to those moments as "high points" in your life, times when you were "clear," "felt great," or however you would describe that experience.

The Ancient Greeks had a word, in the sport of archery, for the distance between the center of a target and the actual spot the arrow struck the target. This distance was called the "sin." Thus, a sin is a measure of distance, not something about which you need feel guilty, even though there are big payoffs for feeling guilty.

Therefore, in relationship to honesty, all have sinned, that is, all of us have missed the dead center of the target intellectually, experientially, and at the Being level. To not have thus sinned would be to be un-human. A human being is simply too complex to be honest in all three spheres simultaneously, at all times.

Nevertheless, there is a certain price we pay for being and doing dishonest, and there is a certain blessing we receive for being and doing honest. The catch is, we can't receive the blessing if we are doing it for the blessing, because that is not being honest in the realm of responsibility. What I mean is that if the reward is at cause for the honesty, you are not the cause, and that is not you being honest. It is something more like your desire for reward being honest. So to receive the blessing requires being and doing honest for no reason other than for being and doing honest.

It is useful to realize that there is no such thing as telling The Truth (capital "T") in a world of opposites. Everything you can say has its opposite, and the only reason something looks like The Truth to you is that you have chosen to take one or the other side of the issue at hand. The best you can do when telling the truth (small "t") is to (1) report information to the best of your knowledge,

(2) report your experience as accurately as you can, and (3) do this at your own responsibility.

You can speak from The Truth, that is, The Truth can be the source of your communication, and The Truth cannot be the communication itself. You cannot tell The Truth. If The Truth could be told, someone would have told it long ago and ended the discussion.

The Truth is the context which contains all opposites without contradiction. Another term for The Truth is the Realm of Absolutes. And, when you say that, it becomes a position, a thing you believe which has an opposite, and is therefore no longer The Truth. Telling The Truth is impossible.

For precisely this reason I advise you to not try to believe or disbelieve the information in these books, rather to exist in the Realm of Absolute Value with it. The Realm of Absolutes is The Truth, and these books are from that realm. They are not The Truth itself.

In the next chapter we will take a look at the blessings for being and doing honest at an intellectual and experiential level at one's own responsibility, that is, for no reason.

The Awakeness Exercise

1. What is a "sin?"

2. Under what circumstance are the blessings for honesty forth-coming?

3. What are the three components of telling the truth?

4. What is The Truth?

5. Is it possible to tell The Truth?

6. What can be told?

For answers see page 215

CHAPTER 3
TO BE
The Results of Honesty

*Honesty, at your own responsibility, produces a
direct awareness of the Being from which life comes.*

There is a blessing for honesty, and to the degree that you be
and do intellectual and experiential honesty for no reward, there
is an incredible reward. In order to have this reward it must mean
nothing to you to have it.

This kind of honesty, purely for the sake of itself, has the result
of allowing you to have a direct experience of the Being. Here are
some of the ways that expresses itself in life.

(1) You Are Trusted:
In dealing with people, the garbage which is usually there, which
relates to whether or not you can be trusted, is simply not there.
You can therefore proceed directly to what your relationship with
people is really about, without wasting your time for them to figure
out if you can be trusted.

(2) You Are Fully Aware of the Experience of Compassion:
With nothing between you and others except the truth, there is
an experience of being the other Person when you are with that
Person. This allows you to love and be loved.

(3) Success Is an Open Door:
Most of what we think of as failure is a result of the attempt to
manipulate others. It is as if you have a Propaganda Agency within
you which is dedicated to image rather than truth. When this
Agency is inoperative, the Self can express its purpose in the world.
I call that success.

(4) Authenticity:
This is the experience of being real, of being connected to life
with its people and circumstances.

(5) Appropriateness:
Being honest and telling the truth at your own responsibility has

the effect of making what is appropriate obvious.

(6) Increased Functional Intelligence:

Hiding the truth and setting up a false self requires a lot of vital energy. When this energy is freed it presents itself in many ways. One of these ways is as increased mental capacity.

The goodies are so enormous that it would be tempting to be and do honest for the goodies, and if you do, you don't get the goodies. That is because when you are honest to be good, you are not really honest, you are more concerned with image and pleasing others than with being honest. If your commitment is to image, you are likely to be known as a "nice" person, and that is all you get for your trouble.

The largest opportunity we are presented with in life, ordinarily, is the opportunity to choose between doing good or doing bad. It isn't much of a choice. One is about as de-Personalizing as the other. In these last few chapters I have presented you with the opportunity to make a difference. That opportunity exists in another reality from the opportunity to do good or do bad.

Now, let us look at the impact of this kind of honesty on one's relationship with the other sex. Each of us could fill a large room with people who were once in our lives, loved us absolutely, would have done anything to have our lives be great, and who are no longer in our lives. Not only are they no longer in our lives, they are not likely to reappear, would not want to reappear, and would not be welcomed if they came back. What happened?

What did happen was that the time came to tell the truth in that relationship, a time to clear the air, to be authentic and real, and re-establish trust, a time to tell the truth of your experience. That time came and went, and you did not tell the truth. In that moment of passive lying, the aliveness of that relationship disappeared, and that which appeared in its place was a relationship of pretense.

Eventually that pretense became intolerable and people left each other, probably after a period of intense drama to justify the leaving, or perhaps by slipping out the back door.

Before you read the next chapter, close your eyes and create an empty room. Then populate that room with the people from your past whom you have lost through passive or active lying. Here is a space to list a few of them:

1.   4.

2.   5.

3.   6.

So, what is the price for lying, even passively, by remaining silent when it is time to tell the truth? The price is love, relationship, and loss of the ability to make the kind of difference in life you most want to make. The currency of the price is human being. You can see the price in the list above. Why would anyone pay such a price?

The answer lies in the quest for comfort. Almost all of us have sold out to comfort a long time ago, and rank being, and staying, comfortable above all else. The fact is that telling the truth is un-comfortable, especially when the truth needs to be told. In fact, the more it needs to be told, the more uncomfortable it is to tell it. So, in order to maintain comfort, we create a pretense, then become the pretense and sell our Being down the river. You can construct an entire Personality based on this pretense. The price is love and relationship. The payoff is comfort and the avoidance of discomfort.

The Awakeness Exercise

1. Being and doing honest for no reward has what result in terms of experience?

2. What are six concrete results of a being and doing honest for no reward?

3. What is the cost of dishonesty?

4. In what currency is the price for dishonesty paid?

5. What is the payoff for remaining less than totally honest?

6. When a lie is told in a relationship, what replaces authenticity?

7. What is usually required for people to leave each other?

For answers see page 216

WORKSHEET

Here is an outline of the data in this section, for your review:

Book II: Honesty

Chapter 1: Honesty and Dishonesty—the Definition 45
Chapter 2: All Have Sinned 48
Chapter 3: To Be—The Results of Honesty 51

Insights into my own life which I have created as a result of reading Book II: (If you don't have any, make some up. How do you think you get insights, anyway?)

1.

2.

3.

4.

5.

Actions I plan to take based on these insights, including the date by which time each one will be completed.

1.

2.

3.

4.

5.

BOOK III
THE REALMS

What we call "reality" is a function of our perceptions. Our perceptions are a function of the methods of perception we have devised. We are too close to our methods of perception to observe them objectively. Thus we cannot know how we construct our realities. Therefore we think our individual realities are The Reality.

We construct reality as a function of opposites. A pencil exists by virtue of the existence of the rest of the universe which we could call "not-that-pencil." What we call "love" exists as a function of the non-experience of love we have. In other words, if you love someone, you know you love him or her by virtue of all the other people you do not love. If you loved them all, you would not call it love, because you know that love is "special."

Our birthright, as human beings, is the Realm of Opposites—this is our perceiving apparatus. Things and experience exist only as a function of their opposites. If you do nothing, this is the realm in which you find yourself. In this realm love is, of necessity, rare.

Book III: The Realms

Chapter 1: Paradise Lost—Born into a World of Opposites . . 58
Chapter 2: Paradise Regained—The Realm of Absolutes 61
Chapter 3: Reconstructing Reality 65

Worksheet 69

CHAPTER 1
PARADISE LOST
Born Into a World of Opposites

In the beginning of life, Paradise is a gift. Later it must be earned.

Consider for a moment the face of a child in the absence of hunger or pain. What comes to Mind is a big smile and a happy laugh. The baseline experience of children for many years is joy and pleasure. I call this state of being, which I see in my three year old son, Absolute Joy. Even as I write this he is squealing with laughter as he sprints through our home.

What I mean by Absolute Joy is that he doesn't know any better, or in other words, for him, in the absence of physical pain, there is no opposite of joy—everything is cause for joy. Even faking displeasure to get his way with me is cause for a celebration. The natural activity of a child is play, and in that play is a continuous expression of joy.

At some point on the way to adulthood and "wisdom" children "grow up," that is they begin to act "appropriate," they discover that there is an opposite to joy—sadness, anger, perhaps many opposites—all designed to manipulate others. Those "others" who are manipulated include the child's own Being, who comes to be experienced as a stranger within.

This is, you see, a world of opposites, and left unattended, the Realm of Absolutes has little chance of survival. Remember the story of Adam and Eve, the Garden of Eden and the Tree of Right and Wrong? Look around you now. This—The World—is the Tree of Right and Wrong, the Tree of Judgment—in the terminology of this book, the Realm of Opposites. This tree, the fruit of which we promised God we would not eat, is so large that, when you are in it, you can't see anything else—it looks like everything.

Thus we exist in the Realm of Opposites, which we shall call simply "The World." This is the consequence of rejecting the Realm of Absolutes (Paradise).

Existing in The World, we reject the idea that love and joy could be absolute—having no opposites. So, when we experience love or joy, we just know that we will have to pay by having the opposite, we know that we will have to "pay our dues."

And, because we know it, we do have to pay. We "know" that life has ups and downs, we know that it couldn't be ups and ups. We are sure of this, because that mechanism with which we perceive life requires ups and downs. In that mechanism, "up" requires "down" to exist.

What I mean to say is that we know so well that we must pay our dues, that we rarely stop to be awake enough to think "I will have to pay my dues." Instead, we think all the rest of our thoughts from that certain knowledge. In other words, we no longer think it, we are it—it is a piece of the Self. We think and act in accordance with the unconscious assumption that we will have to pay our dues.

Thus existing in the Realm of Opposites, we are limited in many ways, not the least of which is in the experience of loving, and being loved by, people of the opposite sex. We think of love as rare, we treat it as if it would never come again, as if it never really came before, as if there were a shortage of love in the world, and a shortage of love which people of the opposite sex could have for us.

When you exist in the Tree of Judgment, of Right and Wrong, in the Realm of Opposites, you must take the bad with the good, it is inevitable—not natural, and inevitable. What goes up must come down. Everyone knows that. It is what we think from, rather than what we think. Because this is so, it was a large breakthrough for Isaac Newton to notice the action of gravity in a falling apple. Things coming down is so much what we think from, it took a genius to notice it and give it a name.

Paradise is so lost that we no longer notice that it is here. The World, the Realm of Opposites, seems to be all there is.

The Awakeness Exercise

1. What does the word "absolute," as we use it here, mean?

2. What is Absolute Joy?

3. In the Realm of Opposites, what is inevitable?

4. What is the biblical equivalent of the Realm of Absolutes?

5. What is the biblical equivalent of the Realm of Opposites?

For answers see page 216

CHAPTER 2
THE REALM OF ABSOLUTES
Paradise Regained

The steps to regain Paradise are clear, easy to follow,
and only require what most of us are unwilling to give:
a life which is a Sacred Promise.

Is there a way out of the Tree of Judgment, the Realm of Opposites? Yes, and the method has been known for a long time. Yet because we exist in the Realm of Opposites, it escapes our attention. Here it is, in elegant simplicity:

Step 1: Choose an area of life you intend to transform.

       Example: love

Step 2: Declare a promise with the word "Absolute" (meaning no opposites) in front of the name of the area of life which you intend to transform, in the following sentence structure: "I promise that I will experience all events in my life as manifestations of Absolute _____ (name of area of life you intend to transform)."

       Example: "I promise that I will experience all events in my life as expressions of Absolute Love."

Step 3: Create your resolve so that fulfilling this promise is of more value to you than life itself. In other words, although you will usually be required to live a joy-filled life to fulfill this promise, In fact you would also give up your life to fulfill this promise.

Step 4: Set your promise, and your resolve to live or die for it, in time, by appending these words: "for the rest of my life."

       Example: "I promise that I will experience all events in my life as expressions of Absolute Love, for the rest of my life."

Of course, in order for this to make a difference in your life requires that your promises mean something to you. Most of us think a promise can be changed or re-negotiated any time. If you think that, you and I are not speaking the same language.

So, re-worded the entire declaration reads: "I promise that, for the rest of my life, I will experience all events in my life as manifestations of Absolute Love. I will back up this promise with my life, as long as I live."

If you are not being casual in reading this, that statement will stop you. It doesn't appear to be the easy way out, for it requires courage and willingness to become the source of your life and to have life turn out as you say you want it. It will make how you feel about things, and those little events that send your life reeling, appear small and insignificant.

In fact this statement will reorganize all those events, not only in the present, in the past and future as well. In other words, not only does it work now, it will also work in the future. More remarkably, it will alter your interpretation and experience of what has already happened.

So, it doesn't appear to be the easy way out, and consider this: "The way to Hell is broad, and many there are who find it. The way to the Kingdom of Heaven is narrow and few there are who find it." To what was Christ referring? The Realm of Opposites is not hard to find, in fact it seems to be all there is. The Realm of Absolutes does not exist until you consciously create it. It is thus a narrow path, rarely even noticed—in fact, not there until you create it.

On several occasions Christ told his friends that the Kingdom of Heaven was among them. He told one individual that he was "close to The Kingdom of Heaven." Could He have meant that the Realm of Absolutes was as available as a drink of water for those who would come in faith, as little children, not being arrogant as if already knowing it all?

In saying this, I in no way mean to imply that He was referring exclusively to this reality, and that there is not a parallel reality after death. I am simply pointing to the question: "Can there be life before death?"

In this reality, if a circumstance-determined life isn't Hell, there is no Hell. If a Being-determined life isn't Heaven, there is no Heaven. What I am saying is that both those realms are available here and now—not only available, if you don't create one, you get the other automatically—by default.

In the area of love, and in all areas, this works. If you do it and be it, it works. If you try it, and it doesn't work, you missed a step, I promise you.

The Awakeness Exercise

1. Is there a way out of the Realm of Opposites?

2. What is it necessary to give to create the Realm of Absolutes?

3. How long must this last?

4. Does this work for the past, present, or future?

For answers see page 216

CHAPTER 3
RECONSTRUCTING REALITY

If somehow you could get "behind" your percep-
tions, and see the perceiving apparatus itself, then you
could design it, modify it, and create it, consistent with
the promise the Being gives for your life. In this man-
ner you can recreate the world around you.

If you were attentive while reading the previous chapter, you will have noticed that I am writing to you about the way in which reality is created. Truthfully, you will never know Reality itself, only an approximation of Reality based on how you organize the data you receive through your senses.

That is big news to most of us, because we think our organization of the data is Reality. It isn't. It is only an approximation—a rough and far-flung approximation at that. What you have to go on is nothing more than perceived stimulation of your retinae, the sensation of movement, perceived vibration of your ear drums, the sensations of touch, balance, and hot/cold. It is incredibly arrogant to think that the way you interpret all that is Reality itself.

A thick veil has been drawn between you and Reality. The best you can do is construct theories to explain what might be on the other side of the veil. These theories of yours are not based on the actual data that filters through to your side. They are entirely based on the contexts you have created to organize and make sense of that data.

The first job in interpreting the data we consider to be Reality, is to construct models, into which data that makes it through the veil can fit. For example there are a variety of items you would recognize as "chair," some of them extremely different from other items you would also recognize as "chair." Anything with a low horizontal surface, which is stable enough to support a person, fits roughly into the Context for "chair," which we will call "Chairness."

You have thousands of such contexts to organize sensory impressions. The Context "Chair-ness," serves admirably to demonstrate them. When you see a thing you think of as a chair, you think of it as a chair only because it fits within your Context, Chair-ness.

There are people in the world, for example the Bushmen of Africa, who have no such context. If you present them with what you call a wooden chair, they think "firewood" and burn it, because it fits into their Context called "Firewood-ness."

Therefore, when I say that love is absolute, I am speaking from the Context I have created, which I call the "Absolute-ness" of love. I do not mean to tell you that love is actually absolute, having no opposites, even though opposites are only an illusion. I only mean to tell you that in the reality I construct, love has no opposites.

Just as you recognize certain things as chairs, I recognize all human expressions as coming from love. That is no more Reality than that thing in which you are sitting is in Reality a chair. Nevertheless, it functions as reality and this has certain consequences.

You might say "Why don't you just see it the way it is, then?" I don't because there is no "the way it is." It only seems to you that there is a "way it is" because you have your own construction of love, probably in a Context of Opposites, and you are convinced that your construction of reality is The Reality.

However, when you give the promise, to yourself, that love is absolute, then it becomes obvious that love is absolute. It is as obvious as the observation of that thing in which you are sitting as a chair.

The real question is "How do you intend your reality to be?" Do you intend it to be for you the way it has been for generations of people—to simply take what you get— or do you intend to be creative and make it up the way you want it? Do you intend to be a passive recipient, a victim of the past, so to speak, or a creative author of the past, present and future?

When you give the promise, to yourself, that love is absolute, using the four steps in Chapter 2, thus creating the Context of Absolute Love, you will have the distinct experience of having reclaimed, as well as having created, Reality, in relationship to love. And it will have an enormous expression in your relationship with the opposite sex.

I warn you not to be arrogant by claiming that you already have such a context. If you have never created it as consciously as the steps written in Chapter 2 of this section, you don't have one, and the thought that you do is just you being better and smarter again. That will get you as much as it always has.

If you have created such a context in the past, you must re-create it moment by moment, or it disappears. If you are saying to yourself, "I knew that stuff, I have a Context of Absolute Love," OK—what you can do is use this information to re-create it moment by moment.

The Awakeness Exercise

1. Is your organization of the data you gather from your senses, actual Reality itself?

2. Do you live your life from that it is Reality itself?

3. What allows us to interpret the data we gather through our senses?

4. Why don't you just see reality for the way it actually is?

5. What is Absolute Love?

6. How is the Context of Absolute Love created?

For answers see page 216

WORKSHEET

Here is an outline of the data in this section, for your review:

Book III: The Realms

Chapter 1: Paradise Lost—Born into a World of Opposites . . 58
Chapter 2: Paradise Regained—The Realm of Absolutes 61
Chapter 3: Reconstructing Reality 65

Insights into my own life which I have created as a result of reading Book III:

1.

2.

3.

4.

5.

Actions I plan to take based on these insights, including the date by which time each one will be completed.

1.

2.

3.

4.

5.

BOOK IV
MOTHER
One's Relationship With All Women

Locked into your relationship with the primary female nurturer of your earliest years is your relationship with all women. For this discussion, the word "Mother" will represent that relationship.

Book IV: Mother—One's Relationship With All Women

Chapter 1: Earliest Beginnings 72
Chapter 2: The Purpose of a Parent 75
Chapter 3: What Is a Woman?—The List 78
Chapter 4: Becoming The List—Being the Definition 80
Chapter 5: Taking it Away—The Result of
        Withdrawing the Acknowledgment of Mother . . . 84
Chapter 6: A System Which Excludes Its Creator 87
Chapter 7: Re-creating Relationship With Mother—
        Who Mother Is, and Isn't 90
Chapter 8: The Acknowledgment of Mother 94

Worksheet 97

CHAPTER 1
EARLIEST BEGINNINGS

The intelligence of human beings is a result of the gift to create contexts into which data will fit. Our lives and our civilization depend upon this singular ability. One of the earliest contexts we create serves to divide human beings into two distinct varieties—the fundamental distinction: man/woman.

Learning begins as soon as rudimentary sensory modalities are formed in the developing fetus. At the time of birth these sensory modalities are already quite sophisticated. These senses are vision, hearing, taste, touch, smell, balance, and temperature.

From data gathered through these modalities the job is to make sense of life and the universe in a way that insures survival. This is achieved through the creation of contexts and the filling of those contexts with working, that is alterable, concepts.

The Context "Chair-ness," which we discussed earlier, organizes the visual and touch data which come to you from certain objects, and this organization allows you to label those objects "chairs" and use them for the purpose for which they were designed.

Soon after birth it becomes obvious to a newborn infant that some things in the environment seem to be moving of their own volition, and other things do not move until they are acted upon by these things which seem to move of their own volition.

Soon an infant notices that some of the objects that seem to move of their own volition pay particular attention to him, and he associates those things with pleasurable experiences such as the relief of hunger and pain.

It is to the infant's advantage, from the standpoint of his or her survival, to create a Context called "Human Being-ness," into which these pleasure-giving, pain-relieving, seemingly self-moving objects will fit. Children who do not create such a context are severely impaired and we call them "autistic."

Some weeks or months later the infant notices that there is a fundamental difference between two varieties of human being, both of which fit within the Context Human Being-ness.

There comes to be an ill-defined Context called "Man-ness" and another called "Woman-ness." The next few years of childhood will see intense activity—questions and exploration—to refine these two contexts. This refinement begins anew at adolescence.

And now this child/adolescent is an adult—you. When you see a human being, the two Contexts of "Man-ness" and "Woman-ness" are so refined that you need not consciously ask yourself "Is this person before me a man or a woman?" Your contexts simply organize the visual data before you and you act accordingly, without having to figure it out.

Recently I watched the film "Yentl" with my three year old son, Houston. In the film Barbara Streisand portrays a woman disguised as a man, leading a man's life. Houston took one look at her and said "That's a woman!" After that it seemed ridiculous that the other characters in the film did not recognize her as female. Even young children are quite adroit at making the man/woman distinction.

The Awakeness Exercise

1. From what ability is derived the intelligence of human beings?

2. When does learning begin?

3. What allows us to distinguish people from the rest of the environment?

4. The Context Human Being-ness is refined into two subsidiary Contexts. What are they?

For answers see page 217

CHAPTER 2
THE PURPOSE OF A PARENT

Most of us never got it straight about the purpose for which parents exist. We thought Mother and Father were supposed to win Personality Contests with us.

And, some of us never quite figured out which people were our true parents. So first things first.

You may have guessed, from the previous chapter, that we are going deeply into your relationship with your parents. Before proceeding with the discussion, let's stop and see where we are going and why.

Your relationship with your parents has everything to do with your relationship with all the other people in your life. This phenomenon divides itself along the man/woman line, so that your relationship with your Mother has everything to do with your relationship with women and your relationship with your Father has everything to do with your relationship with men.

If these assertions are correct, and if your purpose is to effect a transformation of your relationship with men and women, then it becomes crucially important to examine your relationship with your parents.

Here we are using "Mother" as a code word meaning "your relationship with all women" and "Father" as the corresponding code word meaning "your relationship with all men." Your relationships with men and women are not things, that is they do not exist in physical reality, as the chair in which you are sitting now exists. Therefore, it is useful to embody them. Mother and Father embody these relationships.

If you mis-identify who your Mother and Father are, that is, if you identify someone else as your Mother or Father, then the results would be different. This is not as rare as you may think. So read on, carefully.

Here is the definition of Mother:

The female person who cared for your basic survival needs before you were able to take care of those needs yourself. This may or may not have been the person who gave you birth, and it may have been more than one person. Write the name(s) of your Mother(s) in the space provided below:

Here is the definition of Father:

The male person who cared for your basic survival needs before you were able to take care of those needs yourself. This may or may not have been the person who was your biological Father, and it may have been more than one person. Write the name(s) of your Father(s) in the space provided below:

Contained in these definitions is the purpose for which parents exist—to assist children to survive until they can survive on their own.

However, you decided your parents were designed to make you happy, successful, and to win a Personality Contest with you. In this misconception did your relationship with men and women go astray.

The Awakeness Exercise

1. What it the real purpose of a parent?

2. What do we pretend the purpose of a parent to be?

3. What is the point in examining your relationship with your parents?

4. What is a parent?

For answers see page 217

CHAPTER 3
THE LIST
What is a Woman?

Just as you made up a Context to hold chairs, so also did you make up a Context to hold women. No problem, up to that point.

The formation of a context begins when one can ask a simple question beginning "What is a . . .," in this case "What is a woman?" As soon as the question can appear, the answers begin to appear. So, you formed a list of answers to the question "What is a woman?" and your list was derived from your experience of your relationship with your Mother.

Notice that I said your "experience" of that relationship, not from the relationship itself. The relationship itself did not, and does not, exist in physical reality, and what exists as the truth for you is your experience of your Mother. Your experience of your Mother was created by you, and from that experience you created your version of the Context "Woman-ness."

This list, to answer the question "What is a woman?" is of finite length. It defines physical characteristics, emotional and mental characteristics, Personality traits, propensity to certain behavior patterns, etc. It includes that women are supposed to make you happy, successful, and win a Personality Contest with you. And, finally, the list is buried beyond your consciousness.

Now, when you see something that might be a woman, you consult your list, without knowing it, to see if it is or not. Before you can think about it, you have decided, and you are acting accordingly.

So far, no problem.

The Awakeness Exercise

1. What ability is required for the formation of a context?

2. From what was your list of answers to the question "What is a woman?" derived?

3. What happens to your list?

For answers see page 217

CHAPTER 4
BECOMING THE LIST
Being the Definition

Having a list is no problem. Not knowing that you
have a list, becoming the list and proving it right—
that is a problem.

Having a list is no problem, and to the extent that you know that
your list is arbitrary and to the extent that you know the content
of your list, you are in good shape.

However, that is true for almost no-one because:

(1) we think our list is right, and
(2) we forget we have a list.

In other words one becomes one's list, or said another way, one
takes an unconscious stand that women are whatever one's list says
they are. It is as taken for granted and as unexamined as the certain knowledge that "things which go up, come down."

When you take an unconscious stand, the stand disappears from
your awareness. As a consequence, you can't think about your
stand, you can only be your stand. So, who you are, that is your
Self, in relationship to women, is your list, and the difficulty is
that you don't know it. In place of knowing that you have a list
about women, you simply know that women are that way -
whatever your list claims they are.

One thinks, directly, from who one is, from the Self. However,
the Self does not think about itself. It only thinks about what is
external to it. When the list is internalized it disappears from
awareness and is not available for examination.

Through arbitrary thought Being creates Self and Self is the
accumulated stands the Being has taken about life. "Not knowing
your Self" means to not bother to examine your stands about life
and the nature of reality. In other words not knowing your Self
is to be unconscious in this sense: your stand is that your construction of reality is actual Reality itself.

Now let's say that you are a man and you are now your list about women, and you meet a new woman whose very nature seems to be a contradiction of your list. You do not think "Aha! Here is a contradiction to my list," because since you are your list, you don't know you have a list. What you think instead is "Here is a mysterious, intriguing female Person. I have to check this out." In other words, this is a woman you feel compelled to spend time with, or said another way, you are infatuated.

Depending on what you think love is, you may even think you are in love. So, you are lucky, and she doesn't mind spending time with you, and now you are sure you are in love. One thing leads to another, a few years have passed, and now you are married and children are showing up.

During these few years you have noticed that she has changed, and she isn't so mysterious and intriguing as you thought in the beginning. In fact, you are sure that she is not who you thought she was, when it all began.

Then one evening at a social event you notice her across the room. She is beautiful and mysterious and you think to yourself "She hasn't changed all all!" You notice her as she entertains the other guests just the way she did when you first met her. Then, at home that evening, after the party, she reverts to being the woman you know all too well, from day to painful day.

Finally you confront her and ask her why she has two Personalities, one for you and the other for everyone else, unaware that she would be the last Person to know what happened.

Here is what happened. She first attracted you, although you didn't know it, because she did not match your list for what a woman is. She was different.

The truth about your list is that what gives you trouble is that which remains about your relationship with your Mother which you refused to bless—those characteristics about your Mother which were never OK with you, which you always wanted your Mother to change about herself.

When you met your wife-to-be you had a mission, about which you knew nothing, consciously that is, and that mission was to prove the negative, unblessed part of your list to be right. So, you went to work.

Each time your new partner acted in a way contrary to that negative list, you punished her in some way. Each time she acted in accordance with your list, you rewarded her in some way. Not that you noticed—you didn't.

After a few years of this unnoticed behavior modification program, by degrees your wife turned up with a new Personality just for you. Not knowing that you caused it, you blamed her.

Why would you pull such a dirty trick on yourself?

This postulated mechanism will explain much of the phenomena we see in the course of a man/woman relationship. Therefore, until you come up with something better, this is it. And, if this mechanism is really the way it is, the question arises: "Are human beings crazy?"

The answer is "Like a fox!" The purpose inherent in the Being, in the area of relationships, is to complete them and make them whole. This purpose over-rides the Mind's need to avoid pain, displeasure, and suffering. And, remember that the Self is the Being's stand about life. Therefore, the Self is pressed into service and the Personality is its servant. The Mind's job is to protest and suffer.

Having failed to bless certain characteristics in your Mother, you are presented again with those characteristics in your wife as another opportunity to complete those items in your relationship with women.

The Being's purpose for life is to bless it and allow it to be the way it is. This fact will organize your life and present you with however many painful lessons are necessary.

The opportunity for completion is rarely taken. Nevertheless, the Being, using this mechanism, will continue to present you with this opportunity over and over. Unless you are very young, you have probably already noticed this.

By the way, this mechanism works just as well when you reverse the sexes, so that a woman will use this mechanism in relationship to her male partner, as well.

The Awakeness Exercise

1. What two things do we do with our lists?

2. When you can no longer think about a stand you take, what do you do with it?

3. What does it mean to "not know yourself?"

4. If you are a man and you become infatuated with a new woman, what happened?

5. If your partner changes his or her Personality, what actually happened?

6. What is the Being's purpose in producing suffering in relationships?

For answers see page 217

CHAPTER 5
TAKING IT AWAY
The Result of Withdrawing the Acknowledgment of Mother

When you take away a child's perfect acknowledgment of your Mother, you pay a large price: authenticity with all women.

If it is true that your relationship with women is derived from your relationship with your Mother, then any methodology to deal with your relationship with women would necessarily be doomed to failure if it did not deal effectively with your relationship with your Mother—not to simply explain it, rather to cause mastery, and mutual satisfaction, in that relationship.

There was a time in your life when you were on the right track with women. It was when your acknowledgment of your Mother was absolute, nothing held back. In your eyes, you had a perfect Mother. That experience comes easily to a young child.

Then you decided that your Mother's purpose in your life was to win a Personality Contest with you, and you withdrew a child's perfect acknowledgment of your Mother. It is as if you took the natural torch of acknowledgment and put it behind your back, then thought to yourself: "When you shape up, Mom, I'll give it back." Therefore, the purpose of the withdrawal of the acknowledgment was to manipulate her to change.

When that happened you began to make up the negative part of your list about women, except that you thought at the time that it would only apply to Mother. You didn't like this, you didn't like that, and you took yourself out of authentic relationship with your Mother.

Then two things happened. She was stopped, in the development of her relationship with you, being and doing mother of a child x years of age, x being your age at the time you withdrew your acknowledgment of her.

Now, when you relate to your Mother, provided she is still living, and you are still on speaking terms with her, she treats you as a Mother would treat a child of x years. She may cook enormous quantities of food when you visit, or she may have a lot of good advice which you do not need, or some other way of expressing the desire to complete her relationship with you at x years of age.

You, on the other hand, were stopped, in time, so to speak, in your relationship with her, and with all women, being a child of x years in relationship to women. You may be 10, 20, 30 or more years older now, and on the inside, within your experience, you are x years old in relationship to women. That usually means that you fear women and you are looking for one to take care of you.

You may have learned how to act your age with women, or even with your Mother, and it is an inauthentic act, nothing more. From time to time immature thought and behavior patterns break out, much to your embarrassment.

With your Mother there is probably a list of 15 things you say when you speak to her, and she has 15 responses. When you have run that recording and she has run her recording, in response to yours, the conversation is over, unless, of course, you run the same recordings again.

The final, and greatest, cost, or penalty, of withdrawing a child's natural acknowledgment of Mother is inauthenticity with women. The payoff for withdrawing your acknowledgment of your Mother is that you are right about her, and about women, and you are going to stay right, regardless of what it costs you, maybe.

There is a "maybe" there for people who see the cost.

The Awakeness Exercise

1. There was a time in your life when you were on the right track with women. When was it?

2. For what purpose did you withdraw the perfect acknowledgment of your Mother?

3. What is the immediate result of withdrawing your acknowledgment of her?

4. Until what event occurs does this result persist?

For answers see page 218

CHAPTER 6
A SYSTEM WHICH EXCLUDES ITS CREATOR

If you were clever, you could devise a system that
would make you right, cost you a lot, and exclude you
from re-organizing the system itself. You are clever.

There is a way out of this predicament, and that way out is to acknowledge your Mother, with nothing held back. The acknowledgment is, in part, for having gotten the job done, for having been perfect in that regard.

The proof, by the way, that she did get her job done is sitting in your chair now. You are the proof that she assisted you in surviving until you could survive on your own. That was her job, and she did it. If she had not, you would not be here to read this.

Your only complaint is with how she did it—you decided you didn't like the way she did it. And you decided that she should win your Personality Contest in order to make it with you.

The benefit of acknowledging her with a full, complete, and truth-filled acknowledgment is that two people grow up in relationship to each other, and one of them, you, grows up in his or her relationship with all women.

In order to acknowledge her, you don't have to like her. If you don't like her, you can go on not liking her and still acknowledge her for what is rightfully hers for which to be acknowledged. You would be silly to go on like that, and it has no bearing on your ability to deliver an acknowledgment.

All that is required of you is to discover (create) the truth about her—that for which you can legitimately acknowledge her. You have part of the answer now: she got her job done.

However, until you create the rest of the answer you can't give a full acknowledgment because you literally don't know who she is. In other words, you are not in authentic relationship with her. You cannot give an authentic, complete acknowledgment until you are in authentic relationship with the person to whom you are giving the acknowledgment.

In this case, you are out of authentic relationship in the first place because you ceased giving the acknowledgment. So that which you want to be in relationship for, that is to give the acknowledgment, is exactly why you are not in authentic relationship, originally.

This is a very clever system which you constructed to exclude yourself. You cannot penetrate this system until you discover the other item for which to acknowledge Mother.

If you were to compare this system to a safe, the combination which opens the safe is locked inside the safe. The safe cannot be opened without the combination and the combination is inside the safe. To open this safe you must literally create the combination. When, and only when, you open the safe will you be able to "prove" that it was the right combination.

The Awakeness Exercise

1. What is the proof that your Mother did her job?

2. Where is that proof?

3. What is the result of giving a full, complete, and truth-filled acknowledgment of your Mother?

4. If the system which excludes you were likened to a safe, where is the combination which opens the safe?

For answers see page 218

CHAPTER 7
RECREATING RELATIONSHIP
WITH MOTHER
Who Mother Is and Isn't

The acknowledgment of Mother does not return you to relationship with her. You must return to relationship with her before you can deliver the acknowledgment. Making your stand that her love for you is absolute returns you to relationship with her from which you can legitimately acknowledge her, regardless of how you feel about it. Making this acknowledgment creates authenticity between you and all women.

I have spoken with several thousand Mothers on this very intimate subject in the last few years. Not only have I not found one single instance of a Mother who did not love her children, I have yet to find one single Mother who can imagine the circumstances under which she would not love her children.

Many mothers object to the way their children express their lives, many disagree on their children's points of view about life, and on the issue of love, there is unanimity. Mother's love their children—period.

Any time in life you find unanimity, you can safely assume that something powerful is operating. What operates in the mother/child relationship is Absolute Love. Remember, Absolute Love means nothing more complex than something existing without opposites. In the case of a Mother's love, it is from the Instinct, that is, it requires no thought or intention to be so, and is, rather, inherent, bound in the biology of being a mother.

Therefore, any expression from a Mother to a child is an expression of Absolute Love, including the expressions to which you objected, and the expressions which you decided were proof that she did not love you as she should have.

The difficulty for the child is that when the child withdraws the acknowledgment of Mother, the child's experience of Mother's love falls into the Realm of Opposites. In that realm certain expressions of love are experienced by the child as expressions of the absence of love.

Therefore, in relationship to Mother's love, Reality is distorted, and along with it the experience of being loved by women in the abstract—that is by all women—is distorted.

The above paragraph is true, not the Truth, and from the Truth, and you cannot see the truthfulness of it until you take a stand that love is absolute. After you take that stand, the truth of the above paragraph exists in the reality of your life.

Until you take that stand you exist in the Realm of Opposites in relationship to love, and the preceding statements seem absurd. So, if the above assertions seem absurd to you, you are not willing to live or die for love having no opposites—yet.

Taking the stand that love is absolute is exactly what is required to be back in relationship with Mother and thus enables you to deliver the acknowledgment which completes the relationship.

In the safe/combination analogy, by taking the stand that love is absolute, you literally create the combination to open the safe, then when the safe is open you can check the combination with the original.

Taking this stand, creating your Self for love existing without opposites, is in the best interest of your Person. What you must give up is being right about your Mother. That is very hard on your Mind.

When you take the stand that love is absolute, nothing about your Mother changes, including that which you have always wished would change—her Personality. In fact, nothing will change your Mother's Personality, because Personalities, as a rule, almost never change.

It takes an act of the Being to change a Personality. A Being rarely acts to change the Personality, and, at the very least, if you are waiting for your Mother's Personality to change so that you can know she loves you, you are a fool. Especially are you a fool when you can discover your Mother as an embodiment of Absolute Love simply by taking the stand that love is absolute.

When you discover who your Mother is, you have the other half of the Acknowledgment Puzzle. You acknowledge your Mother for: (1) getting her job done, and (2) loving you absolutely.

When you take the stand that her love for you is, and always was, absolute, you are in an authentic relationship with her. This authentic relationship will allow you to deliver the acknowledgment for the two items above. This is the only entry to a system designed to exclude you.

The Awakeness Exercise

1. Where, in the Person of a Mother, is Absolute Love located?

2. To perceive the absoluteness of Mother's love, what is required of a child?

3. When a child withdraws the perfect acknowledgment of Mother, into what realm does the experience of her love fall?

4. In the safe/combination analogy, what is the equivalent of making up the combination, from no evidence, to open the safe?

5. When you take the stand that your Mother's love is absolute, how does her Personality change?

For answers see page 218

CHAPTER 8
THE ACKNOWLEDGMENT OF MOTHER

Many mothers live well beyond the time when they should have died, waiting for an acknowledgment that may never come.

It just so happens that mothers literally live for the full and complete acknowledgment of their children. Many fear that it will never come, and many live well beyond the time they should have died, waiting for their children to wake up.

Mothers know they love their children absolutely. Many of them regret that they have expressed their love in the way they have expressed it, and yet know of no other way to have expressed it.

Many mothers have despaired of ever receiving this kind of acknowledgment from their children and have erected defenses to lessen the pain of disappointment. Thus some seem not to care, or don't seem to notice the acknowledgment when it comes.

For this reason, when you acknowledge a mother, your resolve to get the point across to her must be strong. You may have to acknowledge her over and over again, and make it a way of life, for Mother to finally get it. And she may never show you that she got it.

Any acknowledgment worth its oats must be literally correct. So "Gee Mom, thanks for having me" or "I sure love you a lot, Mom," although nice enough, in no way get the job done. What you mean to communicate are precisely two things: (1) she got her job done, and (2) she loved you absolutely.

So, "Mother, I acknowledge you for the absolute love you have always had for me and for doing your job, as my Mother, in the right way," is a good beginning. Remember, you do not have to agree with this, or like it (same thing).

It must be made plain to her that you know that even the things for which you always blamed her, were, and are, expressions of love, and especially so the events and actions on her part for which she openly or secretly blames herself.

If your Mother is no longer living, that is no barrier to acknowledging her. Ultimately, acknowledgment is a process of first creating the Truth in your Self and then telling the truth. You can tell a deceased mother, as in a prayer, if you know that who she is, at least as long as you live, has not perished.

In fact, if your Mother is no longer living, you have something going for you. When you give the acknowledgment, you can count on the probability that she will not talk back, that she will receive your acknowledgment and complete your relationship without resistance.

Here are the steps to create the Truth of Absolute Maternal Love. The steps are:

(1) give a promise that, in your experience, all expressions from your Mother, were and are, expressions of love,

(2) be willing to literally live or die for that promise,

(3) keep that promise for the rest of your life,

(4) acknowledge your Mother, whether you like it or not.

I recognize that you may not "want to" and you may not "like it." Those postures are part of the racket with Mother and with women which the acknowledgment will disappear. If your mother is still living, someday she will die, and so I have a question to ask: can your posture regarding her acknowledgment stand in the face of death? Can your cup of water stand in the face of the ocean? I doubt it.

The Awakeness Exercise

1. What is the cost of withdrawing a child's natural acknowledgment of Mother?

2. Do mothers know they love their children absolutely?

3. What are the two elements of a correct acknowledgment of Mother?

4. Whose responsibility is it that Mother "gets" the acknowledgment?

5. What may be necessary for her to "get" it?

6. In order to acknowledge Mother, do you have to "like" it or "feel like it?"

For answers see page 218

WORKSHEET

Here is an outline of the data in this section, for your review:

Book IV: Mother—One's Relationship With All Women

Chapter 1: Earliest Beginnings 72
Chapter 2: The Purpose of a Parent 75
Chapter 3: What Is a Woman?—The List 78
Chapter 4: Becoming The List—Being the Definition 80
Chapter 5: Taking it Away—The Result of
            Withdrawing the Acknowledgment of Mother . . . 84
Chapter 6: A System Which Excludes Its Creator 87
Chapter 7: Re-creating Relationship With Mother—
            Who Mother Is, and Isn't 90
Chapter 8: The Acknowledgment of Mother 94

Insights into my own life which I have created as a result of reading Book IV:

1.

2.

3.

4.

5.

Actions I plan to take based on these insights, including the date by which time each one will be completed.

1.

2.

3.

4.

5.

BOOK V
FATHER
One's Relationship With All Men

*Since all men are macho men, all fathers
are macho men. They all have Tough Guy Acts.
This is the largest barrier fathers erect to the
experience and expression of love.*

Book V: Father—One's Relationship With All Men

Chapter 1: The Brick Wall and The Soft Heart 100
Chapter 2: A Father's Job—To Hold a Vision 103
Chapter 3: The Scapegoat 105
Chapter 4: Creating Who You Are—
            Figuring Out Who You Are Not 107
Chapter 5: The Father List—What Is a Man? 110
Chapter 6: Becoming Authentic With Father and With Men 112
Chapter 7: The Acknowledgment of Father 115

Worksheet 118

CHAPTER 1
THE BRICK WALL AND THE SOFT HEART

*All men are macho men. All fathers are men, thus
all fathers are macho men. This includes your Father.*

In Book I, Chapter 4, we discussed what it takes to become a man. What it takes is mastery of one's fear of the aggression of other males with a pep-talk called "I am better, faster, stronger, and smarter." This little pep-talk is repeated so many times that men become this set of thoughts, and think from these thoughts rather than thinking the thoughts themselves. This stand is the Macho Male Ego, or MME.

When you experience someone who has completed the process of becoming a man, the experience is likely to be "Now, here is a very tough, courageous guy." What children see in their fathers, mainly, is the toughness part. A child cannot imagine a man tougher than his or her own Father.

This is simply the way being a Father appears in a macho man, and remember, all men are macho men. In a way, it is a brick wall between a Father and his children and it functions to prevent or suppress the expression of feeling or emotion to and from a Father.

Many of us never discover the soft center of our Fathers because the tough exterior is so tough, the brick wall so seemingly inpenetrable. Perhaps you bought your Father's Tough Act, and thus never knew him for the soft-hearted human being he is, or was. If this were so, your Father's love was trapped in toughness, a toughness that resisted your entry and prevented his self-expression, as well.

Let me ask you this: if fathers are so tough, why do they act tough? If a person is really tough, is there a reason to act tough? So why do fathers act so tough? Could it be that there is a vulnerable Person inside that Tough Act who thinks he should hide his vulnerability?

Does your Father seem vulnerable to you? If not, it may be that he fears his own vulnerability enough to cover it with a Tough Guy Act.

I advise you not to be fooled by the Tough Guy Act. Simply consider the possibility that your Father is vulnerable, and see what appears from that possibility. I predict that, from that possibility, you will see evidence that he is not so tough as he acts.

Be that as it may, a Father's love is no less absolute than a mother's love, and in all likelihood, it will be expressed in a different way, given that he is a man.

The Awakeness Exercise

1. Which fathers are macho?

2. What is the brick-wall fathers erect between themselves and the expression of affection?

For answers see page 219

CHAPTER 2
A FATHER'S JOB
To Hold a Vision

Denied the ability to bear children, fathers do what
they do best: hold the Vision for their children's lives.

You have probably heard of "penis envy"—Freud and his diciples beat that one to death—so I am not going to say anything about that. I am going to tell you about something you have not heard of: "fetus envy." Men envy women in many ways. Perhaps the area of most intense envy is in the fact that women have the ability to carry and give birth to children. This envy comes up in expectant fathers, and since all men are macho, few will admit that it is there.

If fetus envy is unconscious, it can express itself as a medical syndrome. As Mother becomes larger and larger, so does Father, because he is eating to stay up, and appears himself pregnant.

Usually, around the equivalent of four or five months of pregnancy Father gives up and loses weight. However, some men carry it out to full-term and appear ready to deliver at any moment—ready to deliver a hamburger, that is. Almost all fathers experience some weight-gain in the first trimester of Mother's pregnancy.

I tell you this to make it real that men envy women their ability to bear children and give life. Denied this opportunity, fathers have chosen another job, and that is to hold the Vision.

What I mean by hold the Vision is best seen on the first occasion for Father to hold his new-born child in his arms. You can, perhaps, see your own Father standing there, holding you for the first time, and dreaming a dream for your future life, a life full of quality, a human life well lived.

Few fathers ever talk about this. It just would not fit with a good Tough Guy Act. However, the Vision is there, and it is there for the rest of that Father's life. Your Father has held just such a Vision for your life, regardless of how he expressed it. Just thought you would like to know.

The Awakeness Exercise

1. How do men envy women?

2. What is the Father's equivalent of the Mother's ability to give birth?

For answers see page 219

CHAPTER 3
THE SCAPEGOAT

*It is convenient that all fathers fail, for in that failure
is our identity.*

Let's take a look at how "I am better, faster, stronger, and smarter" shows up in a Father's role in the family. Isn't it a natural corollary to continue the assertion "and therefore I am in charge around here"?

Father may rarely say that, and he and the family assume "and therefore he is in charge around here." By the way, I am not asserting that he actually is smarter, or in charge. If he were, he definitely would not say or imply it. I do make the following assertion: in the way most of us play the game called "Family," families don't work. What I mean by that is that the full measure of personal development, realization of one's potential, understanding of what love is, full self-expression, and mastery of the issues of life, all those things we *assume* we should get from the game called Family, is simply not available.

The game called Family is not designed to deliver those goodies. It is designed for survival of the family members in circumstances which have not commonly existed for thousands of years. Families work great to achieve survival. They are not reliable to deliver anything else with consistency.

When something fails, regardless of how small or how large, we need an explanation, one that will allow us to feel that we understand the situation so as to avoid it in the future, one that is brief, and easy to remember. It is really great if you can do something as simple as point to the cause of the failure. That taxes your brain less.

When the family fails, we point to Father. Who better? He implies, simply by being Father that he is in charge of things. Let's face it, he is even in charge of Mother's happiness, and you know how unhappy she was, so he must have failed! He is also in charge of money and as you know, there was not enough money. Our very experience of money exists in insufficiency.

Thus in relationship to a Scapegoat, most of us defined who we are as an opposite of that Scapegoat. This is a big problem for children who spent years designing a Personality by mimicking Father. Such a child comes to act like the person he pretends to hate, and thus comes to hate his own Act.

The Awakeness Exercise

1. Who claims he is in charge of the family?

2. What is a family designed for?

3. What do we say a family is designed for?

4. What qualities does a good explanation for failure have?

5. In the family, what is the usual explanation for failure?

6. Who do we hold responsible for Mother's happiness?

7. Who is at fault when there is insufficiency of money?

For answers see page 219

CHAPTER 4
CREATING WHO YOU ARE
Figuring Out Who You Are Not

If you turned out to be the opposite of the guy who failed, you couldn't go too wrong, could you?

Sometime around 12–15 years of age a Person begins to realize that it is time to define one's Self, that childhood is a temporary condition, and some sort of stand must be taken about who one is. You just can't pay the bills on how wonderful you are, you have to be good for something.

It is a confusing time of life, for in looking for the evidence for who one is, there isn't much. As I write this, I am 41 years old. That is old enough for there to be some evidence for what I stand for in the world. But when you are 13, and you are supposed to know what your life stands for, even in the absence of evidence, that is stress!

Defining who one is, is nothing more than making arbitrary choices about what one stands for, and then justifying those choices. However, no-one tells you that these are arbitrary choices and that the justifications occur after, not before, the choices are made.

For the life of you, you can't see anything that makes any sense about what you stand for. Many of us wait for God to tell us, and when God doesn't show up we either make something up and perhaps blame it on God, wait a lifetime for God to show up, or take a "vocational interest test," as if a test would know more than we know.

There are no courses to help you establish your identity in the world and the few adults who know anything about it are talking even less about this than people who know about sex are talking about that.

Enter the Scapegoat, and you think "I may not know who I am, or what I am good for in life, and one thing is certain, I know who

I am not, and who I do not want to be—the guy who is responsible for things not working around here. In fact, if I turned out to be the opposite of him, I couldn't go too wrong."

So, to make yourself feel safer, you begin to define yourself as the opposite of the man who is your Father. I don't say always, and I say often enough that this is a valuable discussion for most of us.

There is another way to cope with Father and that is to define yourself as just like him. Either way you succeed in not defining yourself at your own responsibility.

Put yourself in the place of a Father, perhaps hiding a tender heart full of love behind a Tough Guy Act, nurturing a Vision for your life, seeing his child define his or her Self as the opposite of you. Do you think that more than a few fathers experience heart-break in that situation? Is it possible that your Father is one of those men who have experienced such a heart-break?

The Awakeness Exercise

1. At what age do people begin to create the Self, that is define who they are and what they are good for?

2. What is the method to create the Self?

3. Who is commonly used to establish one's identity by defining one's Self as the opposite of that person?

4. What is an alternative way to define who you are?

For answers see page 219

CHAPTER 5
THE FATHER LIST
What Is a Man?

The cost of confronting your list about men is that you will have been wrong. The payoff is the opportunity to become authentic with men.

Just as with Mother, one first decides upon a list to answer the question "What is a man?" Then, as the years pass, you forget that you have a list and you become the list. The job then becomes to live your life from the list, and to ultimately prove that the list is valid.

Since Father is a man and all men are macho, that is they all harbor the unconscious defensive thoughts: I am better, faster, stronger, and smarter, the lists people generate about men usually contain some elements of danger—that men are in some way dangerous. If you, in fact, feared your Father, there will be something in your list about men being fear-inspiring, as well as dangerous.

And, just as with Mother, to the extent that you are not complete with your list, that is, you refuse to bless certain qualities you thought you saw in your Father, then you are obligated to bring out those negative items of your list in your closest relationships with men.

This is an opportunity the Being provides you to become complete with those perceived qualities. For example, if your list includes something about that men are violent and dangerous, you may find yourself provoking violence in the most gentle of men.

Few of us ever take the opportunity to go to the source of those perceived qualities and be complete with them, nevertheless the drive of the Being to be complete is greater than the need to avoid pain and suffering. Therefore, the opportunity will appear again and again, despite the pain and suffering associated with the process.

The payoff, on the other hand, for avoiding consciousness of your list is that you remain right in your history of relationships with men.

The Awakeness Exercise

1. What is usually contained in people's lists about men?

2. What part of your list will give you trouble?

For answers see page 219

CHAPTER 6
BECOMING AUTHENTIC WITH
FATHER AND WITH MEN

If you are waiting for your Father to change before you acknowledge him, be prepared to demonstrate your long-suffering patience.

If you were able to endure the previous chapter, you are on your way to becoming authentic in your relationship with men. If you can endure the thought that you may have been not only unconscious, but wrong as well, that sets you far apart from almost all other members of the species.

The decision that he was not doing his job, or that he was doing it the wrong way, was the Survival Plan of a Child struggling to discover his or her own identity, many long years ago. It may be time to re-examine that decision.

To see if Father did his job, look to the evidence. Did you survive? Obviously, you did, so he did his job, and that was his only obligation to you. He may have left when you were three months old, thus creating a space for the real Father to show up, and if he did his job that way, then that is the way he did it.

If he had not done his job, you would not be here to read this. Your only problem with it is that you don't like the way he did his job, and you expected him to win a Personality Contest with you, even as he did his job.

So, knowing the truth about Father is a prerequisite to becoming authentic with Father. That he did his job is the first step in knowing about Father. The second item to know is the nature of his love for you. Most fathers, and most men for that matter, exhibit a brand of Absolute Love which I call Tough Love. How else would you express your love if you had a Tough Guy Act?

I will tell you something about Father, and his way of expressing himself. He has a right to it. You have no right to expect him, or anyone else for that matter, to change. And furthermore, he isn't going to change.

If you continue to expect your Father to change, here is what will probably happen. On the day he dies, he will do or say those three things you could never stand, which you would never bless, which would never be OK with you, which you always wanted him to change about himself, and then he will die. You will be left standing there realizing what a fool you were to hold out your acknowledgment until he changed.

Withdrawing your acknowledgment of him for doing his job and for loving you absolutely, is not going to work. If you don't know that, it is unlikely that you will become authentic with your Father.

To become fully authentic in your relationship with men means to make your Father a saint in your experience. That is a tall order for a Person who has a well-rehearsed story about how Father didn't do his job and/or how he did it the wrong way.

Some religious orders have criteria for who is a saint and who isn't. Some require that three miracles be performed. That man fathered you into the world. You are a miracle, so that is one. He put up with you, and let you live, that is two. When you take the stand that love is absolute, it becomes obvious that your Father loved you, and loved you as much as he could have loved you. That is a third miracle.

So, it comes back to this fundamental question: how do you intend to experience love? As if it had opposites? As if he could not have been a tough guy and loved you also? Here is the choice to become authentic with Father.

The Awakeness Exercise

1. What was the decision that Father was not doing his job, or that he was not doing it the right way?

2. What is the proof that your Father did his job?

3. What did you expect of your Father?

4. Does your Father have a right to his own manner of expression?

5. When will your Father change?

6. What is the purpose of withdrawing a Father's acknowledgment?

7. What three miracles has your Father performed?

For answers see page 219

CHAPTER 7
THE ACKNOWLEDGMENT OF FATHER

Giving an acknowledgment does not require that you "feel like it." You may not feel like it until after you deliver the acknowledgment, and you may never feel like it.

In the acknowledgment of Father, once again, you are confronted with a system that excludes you. Because you have been so righteous, all these years, about your judgments of him, you are therefore not in authentic relationship with him. In other words, when you withdrew the natural acknowledgment a child has for a Father, you went out of relationship with him.

You cannot give an acknowledgment that gets the job done to someone with whom you are not in an authentic, that is truthful, relationship. And, you are not in an authentic, truthful, relationship with your Father because, at some point, you ceased to acknowledge the truth that he got his job done in being your Father, and you ceased to acknowledge his Absolute Love for you.

The key, once again, that unlocks this clever system that you created, which excludes you, is to take the stand that love, in all its various forms, is absolute, that is, has no opposites. That, in itself, brings up an authentic acknowledgment of Father within you, which places you back in a truthful relationship with him, and allows you to give voice to the acknowledgment.

In case you forgot, I will repeat something: you do not have to like a Person's Personality in order to acknowledge that Person. You don't even need to "feel like" giving the acknowledgment to give it. In order to acknowledge a person you have only to pronounce the words.

If you wish, you can go on not liking his Personality, and wishing he would change, which, of course, he never will. You would be a fool to do so, however, it is not necessary that you change your point of view about his Personality in order to acknowledge him.

The acknowledgment that works may not be deliverable on one

occasion. You have probably made such a fool of yourself, in your Father's eyes, that he will not believe you woke up. You may have to repeat it over and over until he sees that he is facing the genuine article of acknowledgment. I required five years to fully deliver my Father's acknowledgment to his satisfaction, so that he knew I had finally awakened.

Many fathers wait a life-time, and some live long beyond the time of their natural death, awaiting this acknowledgment. It is the one thing a Father wants more than anything in the world, and many fathers go to their graves without it. If you are going to do it, do it now, do not procrastinate.

In case your Father is no longer living, that is no problem. Acknowledge him, as in a prayer. Acknowledgment is a process of telling the truth within you, and you can do this just as well in a prayer. If he is living, voice the acknowledgment to him directly, in person, in writing, or by telephone, until you see that he got it.

I wish to emphasize that to begin the process of acknowledgment does not require that you feel like it. You may feel very unlike it, and begin anyway. If the stand you take that love is absolute is not stronger than your feelings, you didn't take the stand. And, when you direct your life, your feelings eventually align with your direction. The acknowledgment you give will initiate a process which will eventually lead to you "feeling like it," and that is not the point.

If your Father is still living, one day he will die. Can your refusal to acknowledge him stand in the face of death?

The Awakeness Exercise

1. What is required to be able to deliver an acknowledgment that works?

2. How is that achieved?

3. Is it necessary for you to like his Personality to acknowledge him?

4. In case your Father is no longer living, how do you acknowledge him?

For answers see page 220

WORKSHEET

Here is an outline of the data in this section, for your review:

Book V: Father—One's Relationship With All Men

Chapter 1: The Brick Wall and The Soft Heart 100
Chapter 2: A Father's Job—To Hold a Vision 103
Chapter 3: The Scapegoat 105
Chapter 4: Creating Who You Are—
            Figuring Out Who You Are Not 107
Chapter 5: The Father List—What Is a Man? 110
Chapter 6: Becoming Authentic With Father and With Men 112
Chapter 7: The Acknowledgment of Father 115

Insights into my own life which I have created as a result of reading Book V:

1.

2.

3.

4.

5.

Actions I plan to take based on these insights, including the date by which time each one will be completed.

1.

2.

3.

4.

5.

BOOK VI
PERSONALITY AND CHANGE

Change is not only unlikely, it isn't what you are looking for anyway, even though the illusion that it would make a difference is strong. What you are looking for is what would make a difference.

Book VI: Personality and Change

Chapter 1: The Answer 121
Chapter 2: Patterns 124
Chapter 3: Surrender 127
Chapter 4: The Real Meaning of Enlightenment 130

Worksheet 132

CHAPTER 1
THE ANSWER

If you had an answer that answered all questions,
that would save a lot of running around, wouldn't it?

I know why you are reading this volume. You want to learn something new in order to change yourself and make life better. I have some bad news for you. Number one, short of an act of God, you are not going to change, and number two, if God intervened and you did change in the way you think you want to, you wouldn't like that into which you changed. To continue the bad news, I could care less about a change in your life, and I am presenting no techniques for change.

The entire thrust of my work and my life is to make life like it is. We have masked the beauty in life to the extent that it now looks ugly, and we think we need to change it. I have no changes to propose, rather I propose that we see life as it already is, that we unmask the lies about life. This is the meaning of transformation. It doesn't negate change, for change is itself unchanging. Transformation merely exists in another realm from change, and its thrust is to make life authentic, not change it.

Any book that aspires to provide people an opportunity to transform an area of life is necessarily invalid unless the author emphasizes The Answer. What I mean by The Answer, with capital letters, is that Answer which will serve, throughout life, as a source for answers to all the questions of life.

Let's face it, at least a chance of finding The Answer is the only purpose which could possibly make it worth-while for you to spend your money and time to buy and read this volume. Fact is, many people will pass up this volume because they have been disappointed with so many books before, simply because The Answer was not there.

I know, therefore, why you bought this volume, and why you are studying it so carefully. It is the same reason you would spend time and money to go to a seminar, workshop, or training—to get The Answer.

It is really incredible—people will go anywhere, spend any amount of money, do anything to get a chance at The Answer. That The Answer doesn't show up will not deter them from doing it again. I have seen seminar leaders do nothing other than change the name of their seminar to get graduates to take it again. As for myself, I just add an extra day, and here they come again.

If you look at the content of this volume, there are some good candidates for The Answer, Absolute Love for example. Or, perhaps Honesty, or Completion of Relationships, or a number of other items still to come. None of these are It. They are only from It.

The Answer is, by the way, the one thing a master will not tell you, because after The Answer, the master is no longer the master—you become the master, and don't need another one.

So, without further ado, I am going to give you The Answer which will make seminars and books obsolete. It is The Answer that, if the seminar leader were to give it to you, and you really got it, that would be it on the seminar, there would be no more seminars.

However, The Answer is very hard to catch. I am going to give it to you, and I promise you that you are unlikely to catch it. You will probably misinterpret it and keep looking. So, knowing that you are likely to miss it, here it is: The Answer is: There is No Answer.

I am not being flip in telling you this, and I really mean that this is The Answer. If you catch this, the answers to your questions about life will present themselves without struggle. In "There is No Answer" there is wisdom and meaning that will require a lifetime to discover. To know this, you only need to empower this Answer to all questions and source of all answers.

The Awakeness Exercise

1. What will it take for you to change?

2. What will people do to get The Answer?

3. What is The Answer?

For answers see page 220

CHAPTER 2
PATTERNS

*It isn't enough to say that life has patterns. It is
more accurate to say that life itself is a pattern.*

The reason most of us want to change is that sooner or later, we
see that life is not a fresh creation, that each new experience is not,
in fact, new, that it is a repetition of some previous experience.

This insight combined with two erroneous thoughts gives rise
to the desire for change. These two erroneous thoughts are:
(1) "Change is possible without too much trouble," and (2) "I would
be happier if I changed in a certain way."

Neither one of these assumptions is true, nevertheless we treat
them as if they were so true as to not require investigation. If you
bother to investigate these assumptions, you will see that neither
one of them is true.

Patterns are prevalent, and common, in the area of the
Man/Woman Relationship. In your relationship with the other sex,
if you look, you will see that you have not had more than one relationship with a person of the opposite sex. What you thought was
the second, third, fourth relationships, etc. were actually just
number one again, in disguise. After the first relationship, the
possibility of a new relationship is nil.

Behaviorly, human beings are merely complex rats. What I mean
is that, just as rats can learn mazes if there is a reward at the end
of the maze, so can human beings learn patterns of decisions,
behaviors, and experiences if there is a reward for those patterns.

Rats are more fortunate. Being less complex, they will eventually
unlearn a pattern that no longer works. We humans, however, are
so well wired with brain cells that, once learned, a pattern is practically invulnerable to alteration, short of destruction of the system
itself.

In other words, if you are a human being, to be certain of ending
a pattern requires that you die. That is why only human beings,

and a few of the most intelligent life forms, are the only ones to exhibit suicide as an occasional behavioral response to life. Goldfish do not become depressed, hopeless and want to end their lives. Nor do they desire change.

The joke is that change is actually not what people are looking for. What people are looking for is the experience of satisfaction. That is not attained through change, rather through transformation of what is. Another term for transformation of what is, is "Surrender," which leads us to the next chapter.

The Awakeness Exercise

1. What two thoughts give rise to the desire for change?

2. Behaviorly speaking, what are human beings?

3. How do humans differ from rats?

4. What are people really looking for?

For answers see page 220

CHAPTER 3
SURRENDER

Surrender is a peace which cannot be explained.
It is a pleasure beyond description. And there are no
directions for getting there other than not to resist not
being there.

If there were a place you could go and buy a change in yourself, what most of us would buy first would be a change in our Personality. For most us, our harshest critic resides within us, and to silence that Critic, we would pay anything. We think if we could just appease the Internal Critic, then life would turn out. Few of us ever look to see that the Internal Critic itself is the source of the problem.

Of course, there really isn't a critic residing inside you somewhere, and it is useful to visualize it that way, for a moment. What does reside within you is you. In other words, you are the Critic. Your most sever criticisms relate to the way you are, and to the degree that you are unhappy with that, you will be unhappy with the way other people are.

In fact, that which you most want to change—the disagreeable part of your Personality—is nothing more than a set of thinking, feeling, and behavior patterns you thought you saw in others which, even though you decided were not-OK, you also decided would survive you. To give yourself a big opportunity to work on those not-OK traits, you developed them within yourself, probably in relationship to your parents, in whom you thought you identified those traits in the first place.

Much of what you are is those traits, and your resistance to those traits, to which you so strongly object. The resistance you have can alter your Personality as well. For example, if anger is a trait you have which you will not bless, you can cope with it by becoming a very, very nice person, at the expense of your own authentic self-expression. In other words, your Personality becomes a pretense.

The bottom-line question about all this is: "What are we going to do about it?" The answer, which comes from The Answer, from the first chapter of this section, is "Nothing." Given all the above the answer "Nothing," is the meaning of surrender. It is a peace, the depth and experience of which is unimagineable.

Having said that, here is what you will do with it: you will decide that surrender is The Answer and that you will have to change until you are surrendered, or alternatively, surrender until you are changed. You can only do that with it, since that is your pattern.

The real meaning of surrender is in doing all that, plus the rest of your patterns without resistance, unless of course resistance is a pattern, and then, to be surrendered, don't resist your resistance, unless of course, you do, then don't resist that.

That sounds like hocus-pocus. It isn't.

The Awakeness Exercise

1. Who is your harshest critic (maybe)?

2. What do you want to do about it?

3. Where did the disagreeable parts of your Personality come from in the first place?

4. What is there to do about your Personality?

5. In relationship to whom did you develop most of your Personality?

6. If you cope with your Personality by resisting what you don't like, how does that affect your authentic self-expression?

7. How can you achieve Surrender?

For answers see page 220

CHAPTER 4
THE REAL MEANING
OF ENLIGHTENMENT

Real enlightenment is simple and easy to understand. That guru hocus-pocus will give you problems, however.

Now, after the above discussion, is an opportune time to clear up this business of enlightenment. It is useful, indeed, to discover your own enlightenment in relationship to the other sex, as well as in the rest of your life (of course, when you consider what the Man/Woman Relationship includes, there isn't much left for the "rest").

If I wanted to get a big following, (and I know a few who have), I would tell you that there was a time when I saw a big flash of light from God and that life has never been the same for me. That would not only be a lie, it would be a con as well, and worse, it would be worthless to you, unless I could tell you how to get your own big flash of light. Gurus are great at having seen a big flash of light, and a little weak in telling others how to achieve their own big flash.

Real enlightenment is nothing more than a hearty, and frequently occurring, laugh at the Game of Life, beginning with the Game called "Your Life." If the first three chapters of this section are not an occasion for a hearty laugh at yourself—a Personality bent on change which cannot change—then you may be beyond hope. You can't even change the belief that you can change—that is funny!

When you know that the universe is an incredible joke, not a derisive joke without respect, and a hilarious, continuing, joke, of which you are the punch-line, then you are enlightened. And that is all there is to it. Until now, those who knew weren't telling, because if they told that would be the end of their guruship. I don't mind telling you, because I never wanted to be your guru anyway.

The Awakeness Exercise

1. What is real enlightenment?

For answer see page 221

WORKSHEET

Here is an outline of the data in this section, for your review:

Book VI: Personality and Change

Chapter 1: The Answer 121
Chapter 2: Patterns 124
Chapter 3: Surrender 127
Chapter 4: Enlightenment 130

Insights into my own life which I have created as a result of reading Book VI:

1.

2.

3.

4.

5.

Actions I plan to take based on these insights, including the date by which time each one will be completed.

1.

2.

3.

4.

5.

BOOK VII
TELLING IT LIKE IT IS

You will not like to hear it the way it is.
The only way to make it tolerable is to realize
how incredibly funny it is.

Book VII: Telling It Like It Is

Chapter 1: The Club—Domination 135
Chapter 2: The Auxiliary—Mean—
           The Price for Domination 138
Chapter 3: The Potential for Violence—The Real Issue 141
Chapter 4: The Role of Fairy Tales 144
Chapter 5: What Every Man Searches For—
           A Nice Virgin Princess 147
Chapter 6: What Every Woman Searches For—
           A Non-Macho Prince 150

Worksheet 152

CHAPTER 1
THE CLUB
Domination

*Men dominate women. If you have failed to notice
that, you should come back from lunch.*

In case you have not noticed, men dominate women. If you have
failed to noticed that, you are either not paying attention, you
haven't been around very long, or you are living in a fairy tale. Also,
in case you have not noticed, women are quite unhappy about it.
(More about that in the next chapter)

It is as if every man were carrying a Card which entitled him
to travel anywhere in the world and enjoy certain privileges simply
by virtue of being a man. If you are born male, you are born with
this Calling Card, and, unlike your other cards, it cannot be lost.
You need not show it. In fact, it is considered indiscreet if you show
it. You have only to look like you have one. This Card is nothing
more than a tag of tissue with which every man was born. By
appearing to have one of these Cards, by almost unanimous con-
sent, men have privilege.

If you are a man, try this: walk into a hotel with a woman. Who
is expected to register? To whom does the bell-boy relate, and who
is ignored. Or, walk into a restaurant with a woman. Who is
expected to choose a table. Who tastes the wine to see if it is OK?
Who is assumed to have the money, and thus receives the check?
This kind of privilege is so ingrained in the cultures of the world,
we do not need to think, in fact it is better not to think, in order
to receive it.

Men Dominate women—economically. Try being a woman
applying for a credit card. Take a look at the fact that after 20, and
more, years of militant feminism, men still make significantly more
money than women for the same work. Consider that the voca-
tions which are dominated by women, such as teaching, nursing,
child-care, are still the lowest paid professions available.

Men, listen up! Women are angry about the issue of men and

money—much more angry than you have suspected. Do you know that, in the U. S. right now, 70% of the people below the official poverty line are female? That is even greater than 20 years ago! Women are angry, gentlemen, with good reason, and this anger will show up in your relationships with women, I promise you.

Obviously, there is a conspiracy of sorts afoot, and it is nothing new. It has been around for many thousands of years, since the dawn of technology. It is as if all men have a special relationship with each other, the purpose of which is to maintain male dominance, and thus privilege. I don't mean to say that this is a conscious conspiracy, as if all men took an oath of membership and a vow of secrecy. It is much more subtle than that, thus more powerful, and less likely to change.

I choose to call this unconscious relationship all men share, the purpose of which is to maintain privilege, The Club. To be a member of The Club, it is only required that you become a man. As we have seen, all boys become men by becoming the thoughts "I am better, faster, stronger, and smarter." (See Book I, Chapter IV) So, the purpose of The Club is to maintain privilege—and all men are members. Boys are not members, and in fact, The Club makes no distinction between boys and girls—they are all children in the eyes of The Club.

There is a history behind The Club, and we will save it for later. (See Book VIII, Chapter 4) For now, it is only necessary to notice, without too much resistance from your case, that men dominate women. I don't mean to judge it, say that we should change it, or be indignant about it. For now just notice that I assert it to be true.

The Awakeness Exercise

1. In what ways do men dominate women?

2. What do we call the relationship all men have have with each other, the purpose of which is to maintain privilege?

3. Who qualifies for membership in The Club?

4. What is a "man?"

For answers see page 221

CHAPTER 2
THE AUXILIARY
Mean—The Price for Domination

Women outsmart men, all day, every day. Even so,
men, thinking they are smarter, haven't noticed.
The greatest mystery about men, for women, is how
men can be that stupid.

Every woman has noticed the facts of the previous chapter. Each woman could have written that chapter—in her own words, of course. It was written for men, not for women. Each woman has not only noticed the domination which is going on, each woman has, in fact, done something about it, or is planning to do something about it.

What women have done is form a much more conscious organization to cope with The Club, and every women is a member. Because this organization is a response to The Club, I will term it The Auxiliary. All women are Sisters in The Auxiliary, just as all men are Brothers in The Club.

To be a member of The Auxiliary requires that one be a woman. Girls do not qualify. While men become a macho stance to gain membership in The Club, women become members of The Auxiliary simply by noticing what men are up to. Between all women who have noticed this, there is a special relationship into which no man is invited.

Women have not sat idly by while men have been maintaining privilege. The Auxiliary is designed to support individual women in extracting a just price from individual men for the mere existence of The Club. This price is wrapped up in the word "Mean." Mean is short for any act of revenge on a man, carried out by a woman, out of the resentment woman have for men being men and maintaining privilege. That accounts for almost all the revenge women take out on men.

So, in an intimate relationship, individual men pay a price at the hands of individual women for the existence of The Club. To pay this price, an individual man must do nothing other than be a man. (This explains a lot doesn't it men?) But, when do men pay this price? Definitely not in the beginning of a relationship.

At the beginning of a relationship there is an issue called trust, or the lack thereof. Women know what men want, much more than men know what women want. Women know, for example, that a man is not looking for a mean woman, quite the contrary. He is looking for a nice woman, as if there is one somewhere.

So, in the beginning of a man/woman relationship, before she trusts him not to leave, she is laying a lot of Nice on him. This is powerful stuff for any man who has been around long enough to know that there are more than a few mean woman out there, and not long enough to discover there to be no other kind of woman.

So, the relationship progresses, and he makes many declarations of love. Then the evidence that he loves her, which she will accept, comes along—probably he commits to her that which is most precious to him—his property. As she becomes progressively certain that he will stay, she feels safe enough in his love and devotion to share with him the anger which was always there for her. This anger may not be directed at him personally, and in the way it is expressed it might as well be.

As time passes, and the Mean becomes more pronounced, he begins to think about leaving. The woman has a choice at this point to modulate the Mean or accelerate it. This choice is her vote as to whether to keep him or not, for if she modulates the Mean, she can keep him on a string indefinitely. If she accelerates the Mean, he will leave. In fact this is a woman's favorite method of getting rid of a man, and have him think that it was his decision to leave.

Here is what a man is in relationship to a woman—a simple machine which evaluates how much Nice / how much Mean he is getting and decides to stay or leave based on that, and not much else.

Men actually think that when a woman is mean, it signifies that she doesn't love him. The truth is that when a woman is mean to a man it indicates that she has chosen him to love, and that she trusts him more than she trusts other men. A man should worry when his woman stops being mean, and really worry when she starts being mean to the guy next door.

The Awakeness Exercise

1. What do we call the relationship all women have with each other who have noticed what The Club is up to?

2. What is Mean?

3. What do men get a lot of in the beginning of a relationship?

4. When does Nice turn to Mean?

5. How can a woman keep a man?

6. How can a woman get rid of a man?

7. How do men interpret Mean?

For answers see page 221

CHAPTER 3
THE POTENTIAL FOR VIOLENCE
The Real Issue

Men dominate women out of the very fact of superior size and strength. No action is necessary.

When you see this Club / Auxiliary relationship for what it is, you may have questions about how all this could ever have come to pass. The origin of the Club / Auxiliary relationship is buried deep in the history of humankind, and we will look at its origins closely, later. (Book VIII, Chapters 4 and 5) Suffice it to say, at this time, that the potential for violence has something to do with it.

There is a myth that men dominate women because men have a certain kind of external genitals which women do not have. What men *think* is that they are smarter and can thus dominate women. Nothing could be further from the truth. Make no mistake about it, men dominate women because men are bigger and stronger than women, and that is the only circumstance behind this situation. It isn't the penis, it is the bicep muscle.

Men are not required to overtly use this strength and size advantage, precisely because it is so pronounced. If men and women were close to the same size and strength, there would be a lot more violence between the sexes. However, the potential for violence is always there.

Civilized men have difficulty understanding the fear women have of men. It is the same fear every boy experienced when confronted with the bigger, stronger, meaner bully in grade school. Maybe he didn't beat you up, and he could have.

So women, in their fear of violence, have devised the Mean Method to even the score. And it is evened, not approximately, but with great precision. Men reap what they sow, it is just that men are too stupid to know it.

Women have difficulty believing that men don't know that. In fact, women do not believe that men know as little as they do about the Man/Woman Relationship. Women think that men are playing dumb—just faking it as a way of being irresponsible.

The biggest news in this discussion for women is that men really are that dumb. We are not faking it. About as smart as any man ever becomes about the Man/Woman Relationship is an appreciation of the depth of his own stupidity. And there are no exceptions. Make no mistake about it: any woman, who wants to, can outsmart any man who lives, given half a chance. A word to the wise, gentlemen.

The Awakeness Exercise

1. What is the basis for male domination of women?

2. What is the popular myth about how men dominate women?

3. What do women think is the explanation for male stupidity?

For answers see page 221

CHAPTER 4
THE ROLE OF FAIRY TALES

*You choose a partner when you are 20 or 30 based
on stories you heard when you were two or three.*

The previous three chapters are pretty much the way it is with man/woman. With that road map, you can walk around the terrain. You won't understand much about the history of the terrain, and until you know some of the history you will have little compassion for the other sex, and with that information you can walk around the issues without a large disaster. That would be called living in reality about man/woman.

However, few of us live in reality about man/woman. It is much more exciting, and much more dangerous to live in a world of fantasy about the other sex.

When you were young, just a few years old, your parents told you a lot of stories to entertain you and get you off their backs, to go to sleep, etc. They never dreamed that you would take those stories as literally true. However, children take what adults say as The Truth—all of it—almost always. So, when you tell or read a story to a child, you can count on the story being believed.

This happens at a time when children are making critical decisions about life. Children decide at only a few years of age how to go about finding a partner of the opposite sex in life. It lends a bit of illumination to realize that we choose a partner when we are 20 or 30 based on fairy tales we heard when we were two or three.

However, in case you don't make those decisions when you are two or three, it isn't too late. Simply go to a well made film, settle back and get brain-washed. I will give you an example.

When I was 26 years old, spending a few months in San Jose, Costa Rica, I went to see the film "Camelot." In case you are not familiar with that film, it tells the story of King Arthur, Queen Gwenovere, a ravaging red-head, and Lancelot du Lac. Lancelot and Gwenovere fall madly in love and their relationship leads to

144

great unhappiness.

The next day I met, seemingly by happen-stance, the most beautiful red-headed woman—married of course—I have ever seen. I was severely infatuated with her and spent one year of my life playing out this little drama. Do you know how hard it is to find a red-head in Costa Rica?

So, if you miss out on the fairy tales when you are two or three years old, not to worry—you still have time to make a real fool of yourself. It's never too late. Go see Camelot or some other fairy tale for adults.

The Awakeness Exercise

1. What do children do with fairy tales?

2. At what age does one begin to decide how to choose a partner of the opposite sex?

3. In case you missed out on fairy tales, is there still an opportunity to make a fool of yourself later in life? If so, how?

For answers see page 221

CHAPTER 5
WHAT EVERY MAN SEARCHES FOR
A Nice Virgin Princess

A man only wants what doesn't exist. Is that so much to ask?

Let's take a moment and ask a question. Given that life is a surprise of sorts, what things happen often enough that, if you had to bet, you could safely bet on those things happening? In the area of searching for, and finding a mate, you could count on something like the following:

"Once upon a time there was a nice Prince (or Princess) looking for someone to love. This person looked high and low and finally, after going through a lot of relationships, found a nice Princess (or Prince), and, after much debate and several cancelled weddings, they got married. They didn't have much money and lived in a small house and soon after the marriage they started arguing. As time passed, these arguments became more severe. Soon, they were very upset with each other and went for marriage counseling. That didn't work, so they got divorced and went to look for other people. They did not return their wedding gifts. They were very happy with the way it all turned out and considered it all to have been a valuable lesson. The End."

If this were the fairy tale your parents had told you and you went out to live life based on this tale, your life would probably be a big success, if its success or failure were judged on how closely your life approximated the fairy tale.

Now, let's take a look at the proto-typical fairy tale from which we try to live our lives.

"Once upon a time there was a Prince and a Princess. Until they met each other, they had saved themselves for the perfect partner.

"They first met at a royal ball, immediately fell deeply in love, and got married. They had many children and lived, in a large castle, happily ever after. They did not work for a living, subsisting instead on a large royal inheritance."

"The End."

If this proto-typical fairy tale, or some version of it, is what you are living your life from, you can be certain of one thing: disappointment. If you judge the success of your life based on how closely it approximates this fairy tale, (and who doesn't?), your life will not turn out.

Every man is in search of a nice, virgin, Princess. Given that there are no nice women, most virgins are under 18, (thus making it a felony), and there aren't many Princesses left, except in story books, it is a quest doomed to failure. Never mind that. I will never argue that men are smart.

The Awakeness Exercise

1. Why doesn't life turn out?

2. When will any man find a nice virgin Princess?

For answers see page 222

CHAPTER 6
WHAT EVERY WOMAN SEARCHES FOR
A Non-Macho Prince

Fools, fools, as far as the eye can see.

In almost every area I can think of, except in giving and following street directions, women are so far superior in intelligence to men, as a rule, that it isn't fair to judge them according to the same standards. Certainly in the area of seeing through the nature of relationship, women have it hands-down.

Given that women have a kind of intelligence men have so little of, we can't even comprehend what it is, women do have one fatal lapse of brain-power. Just as much as men, women believe their fairy tales will come true. Get this—every woman actually thinks there is a special Prince out there, just for her, and that one of the many wonderful qualities he has is that he is not a macho-jerk like all the other men she knows.

A woman knows that when she meets this savior, he will already be trained (not by another woman, heaven forbid) as if by magic, that he will require no further instruction, and that he will make her happy every day for the rest of her life. She thinks that he will never be angry, always understanding, not to mention great in bed, rich, incredibly generous, and never look at another woman.

How is that for a fairy tale? Almost all the women I know are running their lives out of some combination of Cinderella, Snow White, and The Frog Prince.

Regarding men and women, including myself, I have one thing to say in closing this section: if a fool is one who expects life to turn out as it certainly will not, there are fools out here as far as the eye can see.

The Awakeness Exercise

1. In what area does the intelligence of women break down?

2. What are women looking for?

For answers see page 222

WORKSHEET

Here is an outline of the data in this section, for your review:

Book VII: Telling It Like It Is

Chapter 1: The Club—Domination 135
Chapter 2: The Auxiliary—Mean—
        The Price for Domination 138
Chapter 3: The Potential for Violence—The Real Issue..... 141
Chapter 4: The Role of Fairy Tales...................... 144
Chapter 5: What Every Man Searches For—
        A Nice Virgin Princess...................... 147
Chapter 6: What Every Woman Searches For—
        A Non-Macho Prince 150

Insights into my own life which I have created as a result of reading Book VII:

1.

2.

3.

4.

5.

Actions I plan to take based on these insights, including the date by which time each one will be completed.

1.

2.

3.

4.

5.

BOOK VIII
ORIGIN OF THE
MAN/WOMAN RELATIONSHIP

Many of the reactions we have to situations involving the opposite sex are automatic and incomprehensible until we consider that we were designed to live in a vastly different world than the one with which we are now confronted.

Book VIII: Origin of The Man/Woman Relationship

Chapter 1: How Long Is Five Million Years? 155
Chapter 2: The Invention of Agriculture 159
Chapter 3: The Coming of Cities,
            Technology, and Commerce 162
Chapter 4: Prepared for Something Else—
            Hunting and Homemaking................... 164
Chapter 5: The Origins of Domination—Love and Need ... 167
Chapter 6: The Origins of Mean—
            Non-preparation for Technology 170
Chapter 7: A Man's Jealousy—
            Don't Steal My Property, or I'll Kill You 173
Chapter 8: A Woman's Jealousy—
            I've Got to Have One or I'll Die............... 176

Worksheet: 178

CHAPTER 1
HOW LONG IS FIVE MILLION YEARS?

If the journey of humankind through time to the present is represented in distance by 1-1/4 mile, an average life-span is 1 inch.

Paleo-anthropologists continue to push back the time when they believe that humankind first appeared on the earth. The latest estimate is five million years, or 0.17% of the time since the first life appeared on the earth three billion years ago. It will probably be pushed further back than five million, however let's take five million as a working figure, and see what we can see about the Man/Woman Relationship, which has been developing over that period of time.

The first thing we shall ask ourselves is "How long is five million years?" The Mind cannot begin to hold that number without considerable aid, and for us, it is critically important to hold that number, as you will see later. So, let's give ourselves some aid in holding the number five million.

First, let's draw a line and divide it into five equal parts, each representing a million years.

1,000,000

———————— | ———————— | ———————— | ———————— | ————————
5,000,000

Next, let's take a 1/5 section of this line and expand it to be as long as the first line, recognizing that it represents only 1/5 of the first line, that is 1,000,000 years. Then let's divide this line into five equal sections, each representing 200,000 years.

200,000

———————— | ———————— | ———————— | ———————— | ————————
1,000,000

Now, let's take a 1/5 section of that line, and divide it into five equal parts, each representing 40,000 years.

40,000

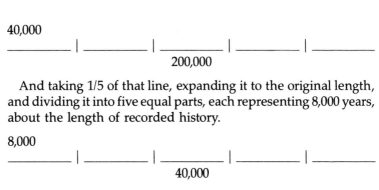

200,000

And taking 1/5 of that line, expanding it to the original length, and dividing it into five equal parts, each representing 8,000 years, about the length of recorded history.

8,000

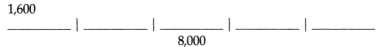

40,000

Taking 1/5 of this line and dividing it into five sections, each representing 1600 years, we derive this line:

1,600

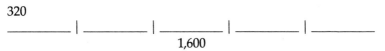

8,000

Once more expand a 1/5 section of this line representing 1600 years and divide it into five sections, each representing 320 years, more than one hundred years in excess of the number of years since the American Revolution.

320

1,600

Expanding one of these sections, and once more dividing it into five equal parts, on this line, each segment represents 64 years, more than an average life-span, world-wide.

64

320

In other words, the average life span is 1/5 of 1/5 of 1/5 of 1/5 of 1/5 of 1/5 of 1/5, or 1/78,125 of the whole length of human history. If a 64 year life represents one inch, the rest of human existence until now would be 78,125/12 = 6,510 feet or about one and one-quarter miles.

In case your Mind doesn't relate to this kind of model, let's ask ourselves this question: how many generations of people led up to the human experiment that goes by your name?

The average age of child bearing, over the course of human history is thought to be around 20 years. If we take 5,000,000 and divide it by 20 we derive 250,000 generations. In other words if you lined up 1/4 the populations of a city like San Antonio, one behind the other, that number of people, stretching back into time, each would be an experiment leading to the experiment that goes by your name.

Now let us look at the breadth, as well as the depth of your lineage. At your parental level, it is two wide, at your grandparent level it is four wide, at the great-grandparent level it is eight wide. Only nine generations, or about 180 years back it is 512 (2 to the 9th power) people wide. So, 512 people, who were living 180 years ago, are your direct great, great, great, etc., grandparents.

This is the relatively recent past. Try 250,000 generations back and see how many people are your great, great, etc. grandparents. It will boggle your Mind. In fact, you will need a Cray Super-computer to get the number 2 to the 250,000th power, and I hope you have a few days to wait for the answer. Of course, there have not been that many people born yet, so some of your ancestors occupied more than one position on your lineage chart. That is a nice way of saying that distant relatives often marry each other not knowing they are related. Incest in your ancestry! In that sense, we are all distant cousins.

Let's look at it another way. If you had a pitcher of sand in front of you, each grain representing one generation leading to you, your life would be represented by one grain of sand, the rest of the sand representing your ancestral lineage.

"So what?" you say. So what is that what you are, and what you have the capacity to become, was designed by a process that in- volved that many people over that period of time. In other words, what you have the capacity to be, in relationship to the other sex, had much of its origin in conditions of which you now find it hard to conceive.

In other words, given the profound changes which have occurred in the human condition in the past few thousand years, the Man/Woman Relationship was not designed for the circumstances in which it now exists.

It is not possible to grasp fully the number of years you have been in preparation. If you grasp that you can't grasp it, and that you were designed in that long process, we can go on.

The Awakeness Exercise

1. If the journey of humankind through time is represented by 1-1/4 mile, how long is a 64 year life span?

2. Approximately how many generations of people led up to you?

3. How long has the Man/Woman Relationship been in preparation?

For answers see page 222

CHAPTER 2
THE INVENTION OF AGRICULTURE

*When women invented agriculture, men almost
went out of style.*

To grasp exactly what you were designed for, in relationship to
the other sex, it is necessary to grapple with what a hand-to-mouth
existence might be like.

When you want to eat, you go to a restaurant, a grocery store,
or a refrigerator. When a quarter million generations of people in
your direct ancestry wanted to eat, they went out to chase the
grocery store which was on fast hooves, or had sharp claws and
teeth.

Frequently the grocery store moved faster than our ancestor and
he and his family went to sleep hungry. The next day, being
hungrier than the day before, he could not run quite as fast, so
after a few days of unsuccessful hunting he became a scavenger,
joining jackels and vultures in feasting from the remains of dead
animals, unclaimed by larger predators. If that failed consistently,
he took up killing other human beings and eating them. (Not very
pretty, is it?) Along the way, he dug for roots, berries, and the like.

When the grocery store was caught there was no refrigerator in
which to store it and keep it fresh. Nor was there a house in which
a refrigerator could have existed, or electricity from which it could
draw its power. A "hand-to-mouth" existence means that you get
it in your hand and put it in your mouth before it spoils. And, since
the grocery store was moving around, and there was no way to
preserve it, our ancestors were moving with the grocery store—
they were nomads.

Items we now take for granted, such as bathing, clothing, and
shoes appeared on the scene very recently, and when they did appear they had no resemblance to your bath, your clothes, and your
shoes. Life was difficult, and in this condition man and woman
came to know each other.

The prevailing thinking, amongst paleo-anthropologist, is that when hunting methods were refined sufficiently so that people could settle down into relatively permanent dwellings, women invented agriculture.

It makes sense. If you are tired of being hungry and tired of your man running around the country-side for days at a time with the other guys, what better solution than to take away the reason for being hungry, and for his running around, at one stroke?

This happened 15,000 years ago or 1/333 part of five million. The spread of agriculture was a pains-taking, slow process. As recently as 4,000 B.C. agriculture had still not come to the British Isles.

So, figuratively speaking, our manly warrior ancestor returned home one day to discover that most of what he was good for in life had disappeared. He became, so to speak, a hired hand on the farm, a semi-dispensable item. He managed to save himself only by becoming a hard worker. It wasn't easy for a guy who was designed to chase around killing things to adapt to hard, daily work.

The Awakeness Exercise

1. What were the four ways pre-agricultural human beings fed themselves?

2. Who is thought to have invented agriculture?

3. Figuratively speaking, what effect did agriculture have on man?

4. When did agriculture first appear?

5. What fraction of human history does that represent?

6. As late as what date did agriculture first appear in the British Isles?

For answers see page 222

CHAPTER 3
THE COMING OF CITIES,
TECHNOLOGY, AND COMMERCE

Man, the work-avoider, saved himself by inventing work-saving gadgets.

The advent of agriculture had a profound impact on the Man/Woman Relationship. Now woman could keep an eye on man, and what she saw made her wish she had left him to the hunt. And the greatest impact of her invention (agriculture) was yet to come. These later events have occurred in the last few inches of the 1-1/4 mile history of human development.

Human beings found that they did not have to be chasing food day in and day out, and could assign certain members of the species to grow the food. The rest could congregate for a party, in numbers unheard of until that time. Thus were villages, and later cities, made possible.

Men were thus liberated to find a new use for their lives, and in this new-found idle time, men started doing what they do best with idle time—figure things out. With a fundamental dislike for work, men figured out new ways to have work done with a minimum expenditure of energy.

There was an explosion of gadgets, and science was born to explain these gadgets and design new, even more efficient gadgets. This building of gadgets to avoid work became the major activity for our displaced hunter, and continues to be his major activity to the present day.

In addition, men not only developed work-saving gadgets as fast as possible, men also made it their jobs to obtain as many of the work-saving gadgets other men had developed as possible. So in the trade of food and gadgets, and secondarily in the trade of a few luxuries of life, was commerce born.

Therefore the brilliant idea of growing food rather than chasing it, made real by women, has created the space for cities, technology, and commerce, made real by men. Suddenly, the Man/Woman Relationship found itself existing in circumstances unrecognizably different from those in which, and for which, it was designed. In other words, you are designed for a different life than the one you lead. Let's see how that works.

162

The Awakeness Exercise

1. Having lost his job as a hunter, and not liking hard work, what was man's new job?

2. What made cities possible?

3. What was the fundamental purpose for which men invented science?

4. What made commerce possible?

For answers see page 222

CHAPTER 4
PREPARED FOR SOMETHING ELSE
Hunting and Home-making

The future of humankind will be determined by would-have-been hunters and would-have-been home-makers.

For most of human history, boys were expected to be hunters by age eight, and girls were expected to be beasts of burden even earlier in life. As a result, boys, in modern times, begin hunting around age eight—by Instinct. Since there are no animals around to hunt down, and it isn't nice to beat up on the family dog or cat, their hunting Instinct is loosed on each other.

This is the background of the bullying phenomenon we discussed in Book I, Chapter 4. In fact, it is the origin of the modern day Macho Male Ego. For most of human history, there was no MME. Men were tougher, stronger, faster, etc. They had to be to survive. There was no need to take a stand on it, therefore.

When you look at what a home-maker is, basically a home-maker is a sophisticated beast of burden and expert psychologist in one Person. The training to be a home-maker, historically, has begun as soon as language and walking developed. You can still see this in primitive tribes. The people who make things work at home are females of all ages.

As a result, a modern day little girl wants to do these things. She may become a bra-burning, women's liberationist later in life, and come to despise home-making, and early in life it is instinctual—she wants to help out around the house—and that which is instinctual early is always instinctual. Our lib friends can only resent their own Instincts.

In no way do I advocate that we should go back to life the way it was. Obviously agriculture, and technology, have provided a needed respite in which people can become what we now think of as human, with the qualities of love, loyalty, and compassion. Certainly these qualities existed prior to modern times, and when living from day to day on the edge of survival/non-survival, these qualities have little opportunity to express themselves.

Therefore, men should not again become hunters, unless that is a chosen pass-time, nor should women stay home and tend the fires, unless that is a chosen vocation. However, if we overlook the fact that we were designed for those functions, we miss out on a vast realm of self-knowledge.

Without this knowledge, and without taking account of it, the way we are in our relationship with the other sex is a mystery, more easily explained by the theory that men and women arrived here from different planets, or by psychoanalytic theory, or other cumbersome explanations in which compassion becomes very unlikely.

Human beings have incredible plasticity, and can adjust to a tremendous range of differing circumstances. That does not negate our history, and the functions for which we were designed. The "race" of the human race, as I see it, is between technology, including the technology to destroy ourselves, and plasticity, the ability to adjust ourselves to the power of this technology.

Make no mistake about it. The people in charge of this adjustment (you and I) were designed to be hunters and home-makers. In fact, the Person in your shoes, right now, was designed to be a hunter or a home-maker. If you ignore that, your actions, attitudes, and experiences, in relationship to the opposite sex, will be a large mystery to you. If you don't see that now, take it as a possibility and I will show you the evidence later.

The Awakeness Exercise

1. Since there are no animals around to hunt, what do little boys begin hunting around age eight?

2. This modern day hunting is the basis for what phenomenon?

3. What is instinctual for little girls?

4. If we do not take account of our Instincts, what becomes almost impossible in relationship to the other sex?

5. What quality possessed by human beings make it possible that we may be able to cope and adjust to a totally new environment, unlike the one for which our Instincts were prepared?

For answers see page 223

CHAPTER 5
THE ORIGINS OF DOMINATION
Love and Need

When you consider that for which male domination was designed and where it comes from, men are not such bad guys, after all.

In modern terms, it makes no sense for men to dominate women, as a group, or individually. What men want from women, in this age, is much more forth-coming from women who are left to express themselves in the absence of male domination. All except the most foolish of men know this.

Nevertheless, men continue to think and do that which keeps women in the back of the Bus of Life. In other words, men do, by maintaining their unconsciousness about The Club, that which gets them exactly what they do not want—Mean—and denies them exactly what they do want—Nice. I don't know how to put it any plainer than that.

Clearly, that which leads men to dominate women is instinctual, built into the machinery of men. The background for this isn't difficult to envision. When there were no houses, refrigerators, or clothes, not to mention that there were no laws to protect people from each other, it was necessary for men to dominate women and in the act of domination protect them, and thus continue the species. Had we not had those kinds of men in our ancestry, we would not be here to speculate about it now.

If you will but look to the creatures of nature, you will see that they know what to do. No-one must teach a bee how to make honey. Complex knowledge, such as the construction of dams in beavers, comes naturally. Buck deer know how to conduct the rituals of combat and mating. Many species of birds know where north and south are and go toward one or the other depending on the season of the year. Dolphins and hump-back whales know many things about survival based on the fact that they are what they are.

You don't suppose that man and woman would be an exception do you? The instinct men have to coral a woman, feed her, sex with her, and protect her, is as natural as any of the activities in the above paragraph. However, given the circumstances in which we live today, this behavior is both desired (instinctually) and resented (experientially) by women.

The point I am making here is that what we call domination, that is the origin of The Club, has, as its source, nothing less than love. Men love women, and as a result men try to do what they have always done to express that love. In fact, you might say men need to do that. It is inherent in men, as much as the recurrence of the desire for food and sex is inherent in both men and women.

I do not propose that things will, or should, change. Even if we want things to change, the drives men and women have will persist. I do propose that, if we remain unconscious of these drives, or condemn these drives as if they had an evil origin, the probability for compassion for the other sex is nil.

Just this: male domination comes from love and need. If you are a woman, and you want a man, this is the kind of man who is available.

Do not be fooled by what I call the "Enlightened Man Act." This is just an adjustment by certain men who were smart enough to figure out a few years ago that the Macho Act would no longer get them laid, and men will do anything for sex, including act enlightened about women.

And, nothing is going to change! So, stop hoping and waiting for life life turn out. Life has already turned out. You just failed to notice.

The Awakeness Exercise

1. What are the two fundamental, related sources of male domination?

2. In this day and age, what do men achieve by domination of women?

3. In primitive conditions, what did male domination achieve?

4. What do men want which they will not have while they dominate women?

5. If you are a woman, and you want a man, what kind is available?

6. What is going to change?

For answers see page 223

CHAPTER 6
THE ORIGINS OF MEAN
Non-preparation for Technology

*What men were good for, for millions of years, is
no longer needed. Women know that in their heads, and
not in their guts.*

The transition from a hand-to-mouth existence to present day technology has been so abrupt, we are simply not prepared for it. Men are doing their best to repress the irrepressible urge to dominate women. Women are reacting in an ambivalent fashion, feeling the deep desire to be taken care of, and at the same time, seeing clearly the ability to take care of themselves.

The usual result, although there are certainly exceptions, is that a woman does choose to be taken care of, and immediately begins to resent it. Nevertheless, because she is, at one level, the product of thousands of generations of women who preceded her, who in fact had to have a man to survive, all other factors being equal, she will choose to remain in this relationship with her man and express her rage in that relationship.

Our man, on the other hand, in reality, is as useless to her as a pack of cigarettes. She may be addicted to him, and she got along without him before she met him, and she can get along without him now. Why? Simply stated: technology.

The time when a man's superior strength was an indispensable quality is long gone. Now, machines—automobiles, airplanes, tractors, etc.—can do practically any of the things which once required a man's ability to develop sudden and often violent strength. Men are no longer needed as they once were.

The brain of our woman knows that, and her guts tell her something else. So, all else being equal, she stays with her man feeling that he is needed, knowing that he is not. Under these circumstances, a man cannot win, so men inherit the role of scapegoat, especially father-type men. (See Book V, Chapter 3) The resentment in his woman is not something he engendered, and it is cer-

170

tainly something for which he will pay the price.

What is that price? If you do not remember, I refer you back to Book VII, Chapter 2. The price is Mean. It is a price men pay for being men by dominating women as an instinctual act of love, in the face of the fact that being taken care of is not necessarily what a woman wants, even though she feels she must have it or die.

And, nothing is going to change! So, stop hoping and waiting for life to turn out. It already has turned out. You just failed to notice.

The Awakeness Exercise

1. What quality, once possessed by men, is no longer of much use to women?

2. Knowing in her head she doesn't need a man, feeling in her guts that she does, how does a woman feel about having a man?

3. All other factors being equal, how will a woman handle this situation?

4. Under these circumstances, how can a man win?

5. Therefore, what is a man's natural role, especially fathers?

For answers see page 223

CHAPTER 7
A MAN'S JEALOUSY
Don't Steal My Property, or I'll Kill You

A man's experience of jealousy is one of having his property rights threatened. If you want to die, mess with that.

Jealousy is the experience one has when one fears loss of a loved Person to someone else. In modern times, the pain of jealousy, and the loss itself, in real terms means little. The abundant supply of human beings, and the technology to travel to where a given human being resides, is so available as to render one day's loss the next day's gain.

Nonetheless, the easiest way to get yourself murdered is to arouse a Person's jealousy. In point of fact, most murders are committed by an acquaintance of the victim, most commonly a family member, and most of these are one spouse killing the other. Need I tell you the most common issue? Jealousy, of course—usually what we call "insane jealousy." However, everyone is insanely jealous when presented with a sufficient threat of loss.

It is certainly true that men and women are quite different, even though there is a modern spiritual movement which claims men and women are the same. Men and women are the same at the level of Being and Mind and can be similar at the level of Self. The Personality, and Instinct, are quite distinct in men and women.

While it is true that men and women are quite different, it is also true that a man's experience of jealousy is very much the same as a woman's experience of jealousy. Both are experienced as extreme anger and helplessness in the face of impending doom.

However, the point of origin of jealousy is quite different between men and women, although these phenomena originate in the Instinct of both sexes. Men have always known they would survive, with or without women. Life, until modern times, could be a bit easier with a woman around to handle certain items, however life would go on without a woman, except for creating the next generation, of course.

173

A man's experience of having a woman, at the level of the origin of jealousy, is not different from his experience of owning a car or a horse—she is his property. In some cultures, women are still bought, sold, and traded along with the cattle.

If another man tries to take that property, the response is predictable, and dangerous. To this day, in some states of the United States, perhaps the most enlightened nation on earth, the situations which justify homicide, in the eyes of the law, include finding another man in bed with your wife. After all, a man must protect his property!

And, nothing of substance is going to change—form may change, and the underlying substance will not change. Only fools and idiots hope for change. The living choose to live while life is the way it is.

The Awakeness Exercise

1. On what premise is a man's experience of jealousy based?

2. Who has the capacity for "insane jealousy?"

3. Where does a woman go to find a non-jealous man?

4. In some states of the U. S., to this day, there is one legal justification for homicide other than preservation of life. What is that
   justification?

For answers see page 223

CHAPTER 8
A WOMAN'S JEALOUSY
I've Got to Have One or I'll Die

A woman's experience of jealousy is the experience of impending death. It is even more dangerous than a man's jealousy.

A woman's jealousy, on the other hand, although much the same at the level of her experience, as a man's jealousy, is derived from a different circumstance. In the conditions of absolute lack of civilization, with its comforts and protections, a woman's life literally depended on having a man, and often even that wasn't enough.

Therefore, a woman's experience of the threat of losing her man is "I am going to die." Any situation that looks like it might, or conceivably could, lead to losing her man is met with a gut-level experience called "I am going to die."

Many men have reached the conclusion that there are a lot of jealous women out there in The World. However, few men have been observant enough, or around long enough, to discover that all women are jealous. As a consequence almost all men are looking for a nice, non-jealous woman, as if there were some.

Nothing activates a woman's mean streak like jealousy. If you are a man in relationship with a woman, and you want to suffer, simply make her jealous, and I warn you, your life is literally in danger.

This is for men to read, the women already know it: a woman can arrange for the end of your life, and do nothing illegal. If you make a woman jealous enough, you may find yourself stretched out at the local cemetery while she is down at the shopping mall spending your money. If you think you are smart enough to avoid that, if she wants to arrange it, there may be no hope for you.

And, nothing is going to change!

The Awakeness Exercise

1. On what premise is a woman's experience of jealousy based?

2. Is it more, or less, dangerous than a man's jealousy?

3. What makes it more dangerous?

4. What is the easiest way to activate a woman's mean streak?

5. What is every man looking for, as if there were some?

For answers see page 223

WORKSHEET

Here is an outline of the data in this section, for your review:

Book VIII: Origin of The Man/Woman Relationship

Chapter 1: How Long Is Five Million Years? 155
Chapter 2: The Invention of Agriculture 159
Chapter 3: The Coming of Cities,
           Technology, and Commerce 162
Chapter 4: Prepared for Something Else—
           Hunting and Home-making 164
Chapter 5: The Origins of Domination—Love and Need ... 167
Chapter 6: The Origins of Mean—
           Non-preparation for Technology 170
Chapter 7: A Man's Jealousy—
           Don't Steal My Property or I'll Kill You 173
Chapter 8: A Woman's Jealousy—
           I've Got to Have One or I'll Die 176

Insights into my own life which I have created as a result of reading Book VIII:

1.

2.

3.

4.

5.

Actions I plan to take based on these insights, including the date by which time each one will be completed.

1.

2.

3.

4.

5.

BOOK IX
COMPASSION
So Missing That No-one Noticed

If something is around, and in short supply, everyone is acutely aware of its existence. If something is missing absolutely, even though it may be needed, no-one notices.

Before penicillin was invented, no-one missed it. It was needed, and it was missing, absolutely. Likewise, we have not noticed that which is absolutely missing in the Man/Woman Relationship—compassion.

In the absence of compassion in the Man/ Woman Relationship, we have been trying to substitute understanding and technique, which all lead down a blind alley called change. The more things change, the more they stay the same.

Book IX: Compassion—So Missing That No-one Noticed

Chapter 1: Compassion—What Is It? Where Is It? 181
Chapter 2: To Forgive a Man............................ 184
Chapter 3: To Forgive a Woman 186

Worksheet 189

CHAPTER 1
COMPASSION
What Is It? Where Is It?

Compassion has to do with the Being. We know a lot about doing, and almost nothing about Being, therefore the absence of compassion has eluded us—we haven't noticed that it isn't there.

First off, let's see what compassion is. Throw out the dictionary definition, for we are going to coin a new definition here and now. Since we haven't noticed that this quality is missing, we do not have a word for it. For purposes of this discussion, compassion, by our own created definition, is: existing in the Being of another Person while still existing in your own Being.

This "compassion" has nothing to do with feelings of sympathy, empathy, or pity. There is no English word which means "existing in the Being of another Person while existing in your own Being," so we are re-defining "compassion" to mean exactly that.

To know what compassion is, you must know something about who you are. To bring forth genuine compassion requires knowing that you have a position in life, and that you are not that position, and furthermore, that the position which you occupy at this time is a temporary phenomenon, housed in a disposable container called your body, which will pass with time.

Your position, although it is located in your body and goes by your name, is actually a purpose. (The Self is a purpose.) It is whatever you have created as your purpose for existing in life. You may or may not be aware of what this purpose is, and it may be something quite vague, like "My purpose is to find out about life," or it may be something as specific as "My purpose is to coach a winning football team." Whether or not you are aware of your purpose, you do have one.

Your position, or Self, expresses itself by creating a Personality to achieve its aims. A destructive purpose requires a destructive Personality, a constructive purpose requires a constructive Personality, a laid-back Personality is required to achieve a laid-back purpose.

Once you know that this position, which goes by your name, and its attending Personality are not you, in any permanent sense, the final ingredient required to bring forth compassion is the knowledge that your Self/Position are not only Being-created, but also arbitrary and inevitable.

When you know these things, you are free from the consideration that your Self/Position is you, and you can exist in another's Being (all Beings are the same Being)—and compassion has a chance.

Between man and woman, compassion has almost no chance to exist, for having compassion requires that you be the other Person's position while being your own. As you probably discovered in reading the above paragraphs, you have mis-identified who you are. Even so, you are likely to go by your name, body, position for some time to come. And there is one piece of this false identity we are all sure we are: man or woman.

Thus men have no compassion for women. Why should they? A man is so sure that an important piece of who he is is his gender, that his "manhood" is threatened by the very suggestion that he isn't a man in his ultimate identity. So, "being" a man rules out "being" a woman, doesn't it? Thus do men treat women as objects for manipulation.

On the other hand, the position "woman" is equally strongly held as Reality, by women, and almost every woman has a lot of evidence wrapped up in a long story to prove it. So having compassion for a man is a pipe-dream.

And yet, it wasn't always so. Children have a natural compassion for everyone. Boys do not distinguish girls as something they aren't, not seriously at any rate, until a couple of years have passed. The same is true for girls.

Somewhere along the line we lose our natural compassion for a lot of people—at least half of all people—and we now manipulate them as objects. There is nothing wrong with that, by the way, and it has a certain consequence which you may or may not want in life.

The Awakeness Exercise

1. What is compassion a function of?

2. What is compassion?

3. What must you know to bring forth compassion?

4. Why do men and women have so little compassion for each other?

5. In what stage of life is compassion in natural abundance?

For answers see page 224

CHAPTER 2
TO FORGIVE A MAN

It isn't easy to forgive a man. After all, men are wrong, and what is worse, they don't even know how wrong they are or what they are wrong about.

The result of having no compassion for the opposite sex shows up in the inability to forgive a Person. If you are a compassionate woman, forgiving and forgetting is a breeze. If you are not, you make a catalogue of your man's mistakes, and remember them better than any computer could. You drag out his offenses and use them to beat on him, whenever you feel threatened.

The inability to forgive, that is the lack of compassion, is really nothing more than lack of knowledge. The content of this volume of books is designed to allow you to fill in vast areas of non-knowing. The final purpose of this volume is to allow compassion a space in which to be. If we do not achieve this, I see no use for having spent this time writing.

To have compassion for a man, it is important to realize that men—that is The Club—are not changing, and that individual men are not changing. So, if you are holding out to forgive a man and have a great relationship with him when he changes, you are denying yourself that great relationship for a life-time. If you are willing to hold something against your man all his life, that is also all your life.

It isn't that there will not be minor changes, and you would be a fool to count on even those minor changes. Who knows? He might change in a way you like even less than the way he is now.

Even more valuable for you is to forgive men, the entire bunch— The Club. Men are the way they are because that is the way they know how to express love. You may not like the way men express love, however it is still love. You have only to take the stand that love is absolute to see that.

It is an odd thing. Women hold it against men that they are so dumb, and men hold it against women that they are so smart.

The Awakeness Exercise

1. If you are not a forgiving woman, what do you do with your man's mistakes?

2. If you wait all his life to forgive a man, how long is that?

3. What is of more value than to forgive an individual man?

4. If you do not forgive men, who pays the price? And who else pays the price?

5. What do men hold most against women?

For answers see page 224

CHAPTER 3
TO FORGIVE A WOMAN

*How do you forgive a mean woman who is also
smarter than you? The only way is to surrender to the
intelligence and the Mean.*

Mainly what men have to forgive women about relates to two
things;
      (1) the exercise of superior intelligence, and
      (2) the expression of Mean.

Rarely will any man admit that he has been outsmarted in any
way, by a woman. After all, men are supposed to be smarter, as
in "better, faster, stronger, and smarter." However, the truth is that
there is no male match for female intuitive intelligence and ability
when it comes to the question of whose way it is going to be.

Women do get their way, and one method of causing that is to
have the man think he got it his way. A woman who wants her
relationship with a man to work will do that. A woman who doesn't
want her relationship with a man to work will simply get her way,
or let him have his way and complain.

A rule of thumb to remember is this: women call and men respond. This applies to two areas: sex and production. The sexual
interaction between a man and a woman is derived from the
woman's appetite for it. She calls and he responds in proportion
to her call. In sex, what turns a man on is a woman's pleasure, and,
short of perversion, nothing else.

One powerful way to express Mean is for the woman to not be
calling and to claim that she is. Nothing hurts a man quite like thinking he is a failure in sex or production.

While a man has no control of how much his woman produces,
men produce and earn only as much as their women will allow,
and not more. If a man wants to call his own shots in the area of
money and production, he should stay single. A safety valve, for
a woman, if he is earning more than the allotted amount, is to
simply spend the excess.

The most amazing thing women do, is to make their own desires in sex and production appear in the man's experience as his own. Occasionally a man wakes up and realizes that he has been had in certain ways, which is no problem if he likes the way he has been had. More commonly, he stays asleep about the matter, which makes things a lot more simple for his woman.

The problem for the man is that he has been had by someone of vastly superior intelligence. The worst part of it is that he had considered himself to be smarter than her. If he realizes this, it damages what is most delicate in a man: his ego. It is a rare man who will forgive a woman who shows him up to be less intelligent than she is.

Most Mean is emotional. The major area of attack is the man's ego. A mean woman will go for severely criticizing those things a man thinks he is: his Personality, his job, his body, his beliefs, etc. It is actually a woman's way of trying to shape a man up and is an expression of her absolute love for him. It is hard to take, anyway.

It is true for women, as well as for men, that they will not change. Only a fool hopes for change. So, when you forgive a woman, it isn't a bribe to get her to change. Also, if you forgive someone for something, that forgiveness lasts for eternity. If you have to forgive again, just because she did it again, you didn't forgive her in the first place.

Remember this men: women are smarter than you and a woman expresses most of her Mean to the man she loves most. I know. You don't like it. You should start liking it.

The Awakeness Exercise

1. How do you forgive a mean woman who is also smarter than you?

2. What is the most effective way for a woman to get her way?

3. When women call, what do men do?

4. In what two areas is this most evident?

5. Ultimately, from what source does Mean come?

6. Suppose you forgive someone, and that Person does it again. How do you deal with that?

For answers see page 224

WORKSHEET

Here is an outline of the data in this section, for your review:

Book IX: Compassion—So Missing That No-one Noticed

Chapter 1: Compassion—What Is It? Where Is It? 181
Chapter 2: To Forgive a Man............................ 184
Chapter 3: To Forgive a Woman 186

Insights into my own life which I have created as a result of reading Book IX:

1.

2.

3.

4.

5.

Actions I plan to take based on these insights, including the date by which time each one will be completed.

1.

2.

3.

4.

5.

BOOK X
CREATING, MAINTAINING, AND ENDING RELATIONSHIPS

In life, all things have beginnings, middles, and ends. This includes all relationships. Beginnings and middles are our playground, and on this playground we can have it any way we want it. When play is over, our choices are to despair or celebrate.

Book X: Creating, Maintaining, and Ending Relationships

Chapter 1: The Wheel of Relationship—
        Choosing a Partner While Awake 192
Chapter 2: The Create a Relationship Game 197
Chapter 3: Sex, Power, and Authority—
        Removing the Mystery 199
Chapter 4: Choosing and Being Chosen 202
Chapter 5: Ending Relationship Forms—
        Its Not As Bad As You Think 205
Chapter 6: Loyalty 208

Worksheet 209

CHAPTER 1
THE WHEEL OF RELATIONSHIP
Choosing a Partner While Awake

*For most of us, choosing a partner is like groping
around in the dark. It is fun until the lights go on.*

We choose partners of the opposite sex for three reasons:

        (1) they seem nice,
        (2) they are good-looking, and
        (3) they love you.

I cannot think of three more foolish reasons to choose a particular
Person.

First, "Nice" is just an act. As you deepen in your relationship
with that Person, Nice goes out the window. Second, "good-
looking" is a matter of preference, the perception of which will vary
depending on how nice the Person treats you. Eventually your partner will grow old and less attractive, by your present standards,
at least. Third, of course they love you! When you perceive life from
the absoluteness of love, everyone loves you.

We treat love as if it were a rare commodity, as if, perhaps, there
were only one Person in the world who could love us right. To maintain the illusion of the scarcity of love, you have to ignore and dis-
count blatant evidence of love. That is no problem if love is not
an absolute in your life.

Given that love is abundant, I want to discuss with you a way
of choosing someone which works, and makes sense. To discuss
what it is another Person could bring to your life, which would
be of lasting value to you, it is necessary for you to know yourself.
So, first we are going to discuss you.

What you must know about yourself is what I call your Position
on The Wheel of Relationship, or PWR. A position on this imaginary
wheel is your answer to the question: "What is the purpose of a
relationship?" To get the most from this discussion, you should
assume two things:

192

(1) you have only one answer that makes any difference, and
(2) you do not know what it is.

You don't know your own PWR because you have been lying about it, to yourself, for the purpose of looking good, to yourself. In other words, when your Mind is confronted with the question: "What is my PWR?", the answer you will get back is not designed to be the truth. Rather it is designed to make you look good. This is because your Mind associates looking good with surviving, and surviving is the purpose of the Mind.

To get the correct answer to the question "What is my arbitrarily chosen purpose for a relationship?" you must look to the evidence—your life. To get to the truth of the matter, you must take the point of view that in every relationship you have ever lost, you were the responsible party—that it was your choice to lose that relationship.

So, if a Person seems to have left you, what really happened, from this point of view, was that you decided "enough is enough" and drove that Person away. When he or she left you, you felt sorry for yourself, and may have enrolled your friends in feeling likewise.

Assuming the above to be true, ask yourself this question: "What was the straw that broke the camel's back?" Your answer will be in this form: "I realized that, with that Person, I would never get X, and therefore I got rid of that Person."

You had that realization at a specific moment in time, for example January 4th, 1978 at 3PM. I mean to let you know that it occurred at a specific moment in time. Your job here is to recall that specific moment and that specific realization that if you would never get X. If X is not your PWR, it will at least point toward your PWR.

There are virtually a limitless number of "X's, or Positions, on The Wheel of Relationship, so let's look at a few of them to demonstrate what this is all about.

A FEW POSSIBLE POSITIONS
ON THE WHEEL OF RELATIONSHIP

(Answers to the question: What is the purpose of a relationship?)

1. My Pleasure
    If this is your answer, you are in relationship to be pleasured by the other Person. If you perceive that you are not going to be

pleasured, you are ready to leave. All that remains is to make up enough drama to justify how right you are in leaving, or how right you are in driving the other Person away. This may take a few minutes, or a few years, depending on how much drama or evidence you require to justify your actions.

2. Your Pleasure

If this is your answer, your deepest desire is to be someone's door-mat, to give another Person his or her pleasure. If that Person will not accept your services, you will get rid of him or her.

3. Family

If this is your PWR, you see no real point in being in relationship with a Person unless you produce a family.

4. Sex

5. Money

6. Mutual Support

7. Love and Communication

8. Longevity

This one deserves some explanation. If this is your PWR, your objective is to make it to the end, and if you do make it to the end, you win the Longevity Game. The "end" is the death of your partner, or of yourself.

9. Success

10. Looking Good

Here, you don't really care if your relationship is working by ordinary standards. What you want to do is look good for your friends, your parents, your children. The relationship is a pretense, but it is an authentic pretense since that is the way you want it.

11. Good Times

Obviously, the objective here is to to live it up, whatever that means to you.

12. Higher Purpose

If some grand transformation of the world isn't happening out of the relationship, you are out the back, Jack.

13. Make up your own—(you already have)

You must realize that, whatever PWR you have, you are so certain that it is the correct position that you can't even ask yourself if it is or not. You simply think all the rest of your thoughts from that unthought assumption.

For this reason you can't have a rational discussion with a potential partner about PWRs, because you assume, without knowing you assume, that anyone with any sense will have your PWR. This exists in the face of the fact that you are semi-conscious, or, more likely, totally unconscious, of your own PWR.

You do not want to know your own PWR because you know intuitively that it will make you look bad. Why? Because whatever your PWR, it is more important than a human being. That is, you will sacrifice your relationship with any human being rather than give up your PWR. That makes you look, to yourself, as cold-blooded as you are.

Never-the-less, there is great value in discovering your PWR, for in this condition you can choose a partner with the same PWR as your own. Being unaware of your own PWR, choosing a partner is like groping around in the dark—it is fun, and you never know who you will be with when the lights go on.

One more time: the way you discover your PWR is by looking at the evidence of your life. In that last relationship you got rid of, what was the straw that broke the camel's back? When you realized that you would not get X, you chose to quit rather than give up your desire for X, or make your partner more precious than X. When you find X, it will at least point toward your Position on The Wheel of Relationship.

One final question. Does anyone ever change his or her PWR? The answer is: almost never. If your PWR ever creates enough cost in your life that you can see clearly that the cost is greater than the payoff (the rightness you enjoy in having that PWR), you might change. However, if you did, you would only choose another PWR which would be as cold-blooded, and as costly, as the last one.

Here is a space to write your Position on the Wheel of Relationship. I know you don't want to. Do it anyway. And, to find it, consult the evidence. Do not, I repeat, do not, consult your Mind. It will lie to you in order to look good and survive the Instinct. With this question, you cannot rely on what you think. You can only rely on the evidence.

The Awakeness Exercise

1. For what three reasons do we choose a person with whom to be in relationship?

2. What is a PWR?

3. How many PWRs, which make any difference, does an individual have?

4. How does one go about discovering one's PWR? Can you simply ask yourself? If you do, what happens?

5. What is your PWR?

6. Is it possible for a Person to change his or her PWR?

For answers see page 224

CHAPTER 2
THE CREATE A RELATIONSHIP GAME

Here is the method by which all relationships are created, consciously, or unconsciously. I suggest you make the method conscious.

Here is the method of creating a relationship with the Person of your choice. If you do this procedure correctly, it works, so you should be careful with it and be certain that you really want a Person in your life. The steps are:

1. Make a List

This list should detail every aspect of a potential partner that is of importance to you. Factors you may be interested in are age, size, weight, hair color, educational background, purpose in life, etc. It should include that the Person, once he or she appears, will be available. If you want your new Person to like you, you had better include that. Be smart and include that the Person will have the same PWR you have. Whatever you leave out, the Being will play a trick on you. If you leave out age, the Person will be 50 years older than you, or so young as to land you in jail. If you leave out availability, you will meet the perfect Person who is happily married to someone else.

2. Name a Date and Time

By this date and time, the Person will be in your life. Be specific: month, day, year, and time of day.

3. Create the Experience of Having / Not Having Your New Relationship at This Date and Time.

For example, the elation and disappointment, simultaneously.

4. Destroy the Game

Throw away your list, and do not think of the game. This is important. If you dwell on the game, it will not work. Turn it over to the laws of the universe and forget it.

Several days or weeks after the date you named you will notice that there is this new Person in your life, and that he or she matches your list exactly.

This exercise will work to bring the Person into your life. You are still responsible for making that relationship all it can be. In the beginning you will know that you are lucky to have this person. In the middle that will change to the thought that the other person is lucky to have you—then begins the drama.

The Awakeness Exercise

1. What are the four steps of the Create a Relationship Game?

2. Who is responsible for what happens after you have the new person?

3. When does drama begin?

For answers see page 225

CHAPTER 3
SEX, POWER, AND AUTHORITY
Removing the Mystery

> *Since a man's pleasure is derived from his woman's pleasure, and not vice-versa, it falls the woman's job to train the man, and not the other way around.*
>
> *Thus, in a broader sense, women are in charge of their relationships with men. Powerful women know that. Non-powerful women say they don't. That knowledge produces Woman-Power. Nothing else does.*

To speak about sex in the Man/Woman Game, it is necessary to distinguish it from the Boy/Girl Game. In the Boy/Girl Game, when one person wants another, the other is more likely to not want back. In the Man/Woman Game, when one person wants another, the other is more likely to want back. In this volume we do not deal with the Boy/Girl Game, even though it is played by many adults. This volume of books is about the Man/Woman Game.

Few people have a problem with sex, itself, and many people see the results of their problems show up in sex. The fundamental difficulty in sex is dishonesty and lack of communication. If you exist in pretense about sex, and if you have an image of yourself you think you need to maintain, you cannot communicate honestly about sex. Conversely, truth is the most powerful turn-on there is—simply telling the complete truth. There is no aphrodisiac quite like it.

Most commonly, men (and remember, all men are macho men) think they are great lovers. This is because there are few women around who will tell a man the truth of her experience of sex. Most men know little about sex, and that is because there are few women around who will dare to teach a man anything about anything, including sex.

Men are like other people. If they don't learn about a thing, they will not know about that thing, and, being men, with one piece of the Self being "smarter," they will make up the thought that they know everything about it.

Women are relatively silent about sex because every woman knows how delicate is a man's ego. So, rather than risk losing him, she will lie to him about how great he is, and when she can't stand it any more she will make up a large upset and thus avoid sex altogether.

So, women, if you want a man who is worth his oats in the sack, here is how to have one: take any man and teach him. First find something for which you can give him a win. Just being there is something you can thank him for, as in "Thank you for spending this time with me." You can say that, even if he is doing everything wrong. So, somehow compliment him, and immediately following the compliment, give an instruction. Then compliment him on the way he carries out your instruction and give another instruction. Do this as often as necessary to train him to your liking. When he is fully trained, you will have a gem of rare price on your hands. And, be patient—men are slow.

Men, if you want to be as great as you think you are, be trainable. The highest degree of intelligence a man ever attains in the area of man/woman, including sex, is that he doesn't know it all, and in fact, knows very little of it. Do not try to train a woman—your pleasure is derived from her pleasure, not vice-versa, so the training is her job.

This situation is derived from a simple biological fact. Women have the ability to turn themselves on whenever they wish, with or without candle-light, romance, or anything else you can name. Men, on the other hand, do not turn themselves on. A man is turned on by a woman. The modality, aside from the obvious modalities, through which a man is turned on is the sense of smell. This ia a woman's ace-in-the-hole, precisely because men are so unconscious of it.

Women secrete a chemical, which has not yet been identified, from various parts of their bodies, and exhale it as well, which has a powerful effect on men. So, the first event is the woman's choice to turn on. The second event is the production of this substance, and the third event is the man's reaction, that is his turn-on, which I emphasize is a reaction—secondary, not primary. The assumption men make is the opposite, thus again demonstrating their limited awareness.

In a larger sense, and derived out of the simple fact that women are in charge of turn-on, women are in fact in charge of the relationship itself, including the position in it called "the man." All powerful women know that.

In a powerful man/woman relationship, the woman is in charge. Her's is a natural authority, derived out of nature and wisdom. She knows it and he knows it. She loves it and he loves it. Nothing else produces power.

The Awakeness Exercise

1. In sex, what is the source of a man's pleasure?

2. Whose job is it to train who?

3. Is it possible for sex itself to be a problem?

4. What is the most powerful aphrodisiac in the world?

5. Why do almost all men think they are such great lovers?

6. Why are women so silent about sex with their men?

7. How does a woman train a man?

8. How can a man make himself trainable?

9. Who is in charge of turn-on?

10. Who is in charge in a powerful man/woman relationship?

For answers see page 225

CHAPTER 4
CHOOSING AND BEING CHOSEN

*Before getting down to "mating procedure," it is
critically important to clear yourself about who chooses
who in a man/woman relationship. You are either a man
or a woman. It isn't the same.*

Because women are in charge of sexual turn-on, and because this
is the origin, like it or not, of a man/woman relationship, between
women and men, one does the choosing and the other is chosen.
Because the sex which does not do the choosing has a fragile ego,
the sex which does the choosing, if she is wise, will arrange for
the sex which doesn't do the choosing to think that he had some
role in the choice which was made, even though he did not.

The beginning of a man/woman relationship usually looks
something like a circus with the man putting on various three-ring
acts hoping that one of them will be bought. The fact is that if he
is going through his acts, she has already chosen him. His acts,
however, can only get him un-chosen, if they are sufficiently bizarre.

Almost always the man's acts are an expression of "Look how
much better, faster, stronger, and smarter I am." Even though she
is vastly more intelligent, her usual response, if she can still tolerate
him, is to let him think that she has bought it.

So, men, if you want to be in relationship with a particular
woman, the most effective thing you can do is get yourself in front
of her so that she can choose you. If she never sees you and doesn't
know that you exist, it is unlikely that she will choose you. On
the other hand, if it occurs to you to get yourself in front of her,
in a sense, she has already chosen you to at least get yourself in
front of her.

Let's be honest about what women want. First women want a
man who is tolerable. Some men are so macho and so unaware
of what a woman is, that no woman alive can tolerate them. Second
she wants a man who has the wisdom to recognize her authority.
Oh sure, it helps if you are good-looking, or wealthy. However,

these factors pale in comparison to tolerability and recognition of her authority.

Men, you may think that you need to be a real worker, a real producer, and be great in bed as well. Look, if you are tolerable and if you recognize her authority, she will make you a real producer, and she will make you the greatest lover who ever lived. That is the nature of her power.

Men, you can listen to what I am telling you, or go out and bash your head into a wall for 20 years, as I did. And, it will be very hard for you to hear me, because you have a stand that you are smarter, and when you are smarter it is hard to find out that you had it wrong.

Look fellas, here is about as smart about man/woman as you will ever get: knowing that next to a woman, you know nothing. If you get that smart, you are as smart as any man can become. If you think you know more about man/woman than any one woman, you rank along with most men: very stupid.

Women, you can go on pretending that you are not in charge—if that is what you are doing—that you have no authority, and if you do, you will continue to bring jerks into your life, like the last one, or the one you have now. Nothing brings out a man's intolerability like you pretending that he is in charge and knows something. Even if you get a tolerable man into your life, he will soon become intolerable if you do not claim your natural authority. By the way, I do not mean for you to be mean to your man. That is the opposite of claiming your authority in his life.

In saying these things I do not intend to imply that men should never talk back and never be seen in public. In fact, one of the things men do well is express themselves. What I am saying is that a man who knows what we just discussed has more power to express himself, his abilities, and to contribute what he has to contribute. Nothing is so powerful as a man backed up by Woman Power. No woman will give anything like as much power as she possesses to a man who makes himself intolerable.

The Awakeness Exercise

1. Between a man and a woman, who will soon be in a relation-ship, who chooses who?

2. What is the social pretense about who chooses who?

3. What is the function of this pretense?

4. What two things do women look for in men?

5. If a man wants to be in relationship with a particular woman, what is his best move?

6. When a man goes into his "acts," what is he expressing?

7. If a man wants to be a great lover and a great producer, what are his best moves?

8. What is the highest degree of intelligence about man/woman a man can attain?

9. A woman who denies her authority creates what in a man?

For answers see page 225

CHAPTER 5
ENDING RELATIONSHIP FORMS

It's Not As Bad As You Think.

Relationships do not end, and the form of almost every relationship you have will end. "Ending" a relationship means acknowledging the truth that the old form has completed itself, and looking to see what the new form is.

Everything that has a beginning, has a middle, and an end, in this life at least. So, when you begin a relationship, you can be sure that there will be an end. That end may be in the death of one of you, and it may end before that.

In fact, every relationship has a purpose, a lesson, even though that lesson may not be clear for a long time. When that purpose or lesson is complete and no related purpose is inherent in the relationship, it has ended, in that form, and it is fitting and proper that the end of that form should be openly acknowledged.

When a lesson is complete, it is complete. You can grieve that or celebrate that, and it is still complete. You can keep up the pretense for years, if you want. People do that because they think it makes them look good, or at least helps them avoid looking bad. A dead relationship adds about as much "looking good" to your life as a dead horse adds to the style of your living room.

The way we hold the end of a relationship is in the Condition of Failure. We think from the assumption that the end of relationship is failure. We rarely become conscious enough to question if it was a failure or not.

The truth about failure, or success for that matter, is that it doesn't exist. Success or failure is a conversation you have about something after it is already a fact, in other words, an interpretation. If you think success or failure is real, show me some. Where is it? I can show you a chair, or a glass, because those things are real. Can you show me some success or failure?

Since there is no such "thing" as success or failure, why not hold the end of a relationship in the Context of Success? Is it so bad to celebrate the truth about something? If something has fulfilled its purpose, isn't that what we wanted for it in the first place?

By saying this I do not mean to advise people to leave each other in anger, or any other form of incompletion, and pretend that it was a success. As long as there is value in a relationship, and as long as a relationship is not complete, I say stay with it.

If you are upset in a relationship, it is not complete - there is still value in it for you—and it is not time to leave it. But, when it is dead in the old form, pronounce it dead and have a proper celebration.

Truthfully, relationships never end, they only change their forms. For example, if you ever had a husband or a wife, you still have one (or however many), even though the form of the relationship, that is, how you relate to each other, may have changed. Really, there is no such thing as an "ex-wife" or "ex-husband." If they ever were, they still are. Rejoice in the new form, and let the past be thus blessed.

The Awakeness Exercise

1. What happens when a relationship "ends?"

2. Everything that has a beginning and a middle, also has what?

3. When a lesson is complete, what two choices do you have?

4. In what condition do we hold the end of a relationship?

5. What is success? What is failure?

6. If there is upset in a relationship, what can you say about it?

For answers see page 226

CHAPTER 6
LOYALTY

I am now looking at that which moves me to write such books as these. It can only be termed loyalty. I choose to be loyal to you, all that you are, and all that you can be. In relationship to people, be they men or women, this one quality is certainly the one most wanted and appreciated.

Loyalty is the quality of remaining true to who a Person is, and forgiving a Person for falling short of that mark. Anyone can make love real, when there are no problems. Anyone can make love real in the beginning, when love is new and fresh, before the story has accumulated about the mistakes made by the other Person. Anyone can love the Prince or the Princess. It takes real character to take a stand for love, that no upset, no mistake, no turn of events can make invalid.

I want to leave you with what love is. Love is not a feeling, otherwise you love, then you don't, you do, and you don't. The fact is you do, you always do, when love is a Sacred Promise.

I know you love your position about what a relationship is for, I know you love what you think you can get out of it all, and that isn't what there is in the heart of the matter. In the heart of the matter there is a Being, you, who gives a promise to love, and who gives a promise to express that love in the best way you know how, each new moment. Sure you will make mistakes—that's not the point. The point is who is at the heart of the matter.

To begin writing this volume of books, I gave a Sacred Promise to love you. I promised myself to express that love in the best way I knew how in each new sentence. I knew I would make mistakes. You have probably noticed them. I am not so interested that you see the exact content of these books. I am interested that you see the heart of the matter from which it comes, and from which you come. I love you.

Your bottom-line opportunity is to make a Sacred Promise to take love and make it manifest throughout your life in the best way you know how. I ask this of you, and nothing more.

WORKSHEET

Here is an outline of the data in this section, for your review:

Book X: Creating, Maintaining, and Ending Relationships

Chapter 1: The Wheel of Relationship—
Choosing a Partner While Awake 192
Chapter 2: The Create a Relationship Game 197
Chapter 3: Sex, Power, and Authority—
Removing the Mystery 199
Chapter 4: Choosing and Being Chosen 202
Chapter 5: Ending Relationship Forms—
It's Not As Bad As You Think 205
Chapter 6: Loyalty 208

Insights into my own life which I have created as a result of reading Book X:

1.

2.

3.

4.

5.

Actions I plan to take based on these insights, including the date by which time each one will be completed.

1.

2.

3.

4.

5.

A SALUTE TO THE READER

It may be obvious to you by now that this is a powerful volume of books, and that I am a powerful writer. If that is clear to you, I want you to know why I am a powerful writer. I am a powerful writer because I have powerful readers, and for no other reason.

In fact, without powerful readers, there are no powerful writers. Until a powerful reader takes up a book, a book is just so much paper and ink, worth almost nothing. When a non-powerful reader reads a book, the value of the book goes below nothing.

I know the nature of your power, I can feel it in the muscles and sinews of my body. I acknowledge your power, and I am privileged that you have lent your power to this volume of books. Thank you.

THE COMPLETION EXERCISE

Here is a fact of life: experiences that are of seeming value do not achieve their true potential for value until they are shared with other Persons. To achieve the full potential for value in this volume of books, create a list of people below with whom you are going to share these books, along with the date by when you will have shared it, and the form of that sharing, i.e. recommendation or gift. If you don't want to do it, do it anyway.

	Person	Date	Form
1.			
2.			
3.			
4.			
5.			
6.			
7.			
8.			
9.			
10.			
11.			
12.			

WHERE TO GO FROM HERE

If you have diligently read these books, and completed all the exercises, what you can expect to appear is mastery in your relationship with the opposite sex if, and only if, you do not make a belief system of the information in these books, and if, and only if, mastery was your intended purpose in reading. Once you have read each page completely and done all the exercises, you should set this volume down and not read it again until you are ready for the next level of mastery. Then, you should read it cover to cover, and do all the exercises as if there had never been a first reading.

Remember, on the road to mastery is acceleration and upset, the two results I promised you in the beginning. How long does mastery require? For me it was 20 years. You may not be as slow as I am. Remember who is the great teacher: Life, herself. All other teachers are her hand-maidens.

THE EMPOWERING MAN/WOMAN RELATIONSHIP TRAINING

To bring The Empowering Man/Woman Relationship Training to your community, contact Ron Smothermon directly.

The Man/Woman Institute
P.O. Box 2909
Rohnert Park, CA 94928-6506
(707) 584-4423

THE ANSWERS
TO THE AWAKENESS EXERCISE QUESTIONS

Book I, Chapter 1
Pages 21–24

1. The relationship all men have with all women and all women have with all men in whose boundaries individual man/woman relationships are confined and express themselves
2. Instinctual and spiritual
3. Spiritual can change, instinctual cannot
4. Five million years
5. According to the mastery it provides in living life

Book I, Chapter 2
Pages 25–27

1. Stay alive.
2. The Man/Woman Game
3. Sex
4. Integration into the rest of your life
5. Comfort, joy, happiness, respect

Book I, Chapter 3
Pages 28–31

1. Yes. Nuclear holocaust
2. Yes. By accident
3. Sufficient time
4. Hunger and war and the means to end both
5. Nuclear holocaust

Book I, Chapter 4
Pages 32–35

1. The Macho Male Ego
2. The Macho Male Ego
3. Simulate a Macho Male Ego
4. The four unconscious thoughts: I am better, faster, stronger, and smarter
5. Control of fear in a male child in order to function and learn
6. Eight to 18
7. None

Book I, Chapter 5
Pages 36–38

1. The ability to find solutions to conflict without resort to violence or domination by threat of violence
2. The back
3. The possibility of violence and the fact that men are stronger
4. "I must have a man, or I am going to die."
5. Innumerable generations of female ancestors for whom the thought was true
6. Alone, at night
7. What factors keep the Feminine Principle in the back of the Bus of Life?

Book I, Chapter 6
Pages 39–41

1. The notion that no-one makes a difference
2. Recognition, acknowledgment, and credit
3. All intersections shift
4. The reality of death

Book II, Chapter 1
Pages 45–47

1. Passive—something you don't do
2. Active and passive
3. Do not lie and actively tell the truth.
4. Do honest for no reward.
5. When it is time to tell the truth, remain passive and/or tell lies.
6. Tell the truth, or lie, or remain silent to manipulate life, to get a reward, etc.

Book II, Chapter 2
Pages 48–50

1. The distance between the center of a target and the actual point an arrow strikes the target
2. Under the circumstances that you are being and doing honest for no reward
3. (1) accurate information, (2) tell truth of your experience, (3) do numbers 1 and 2 at your own responsibility for no reward

4. It doesn't exist—that is it isn't a thing. Alternatively, it is the context which contains opposites without contradiction.
5. No, The Truth is unspeakable.
6. Your perception of the facts

Book II, Chapter 3
Pages 51–54

1. A direct experience of the Being
2. (1) Trust
   (2) Compassion
   (3) Success
   (4) Authenticity
   (5) Appropriateness
   (6) Increased functional intelligence
3. Loss of aliveness in relationships
4. Human beings
5. Comfort
6. Pretense
7. Drama

Book III, Chapter 1
Pages 58–60

1. Having no opposites
2. Joy, of which all experience is an expression
3. We have to "pay the price."
4. The Garden of Eden
5. The World or, Hell

Book III, Chapter 2
Pages 61–64

1. Yes.
2. A certain kind of promise
3. Your life-time
4. All three

Book III, Chapter 3
Pages 65–68

1. No.
2. Yes.

3. The contexts we create
4. There is no such thing.
5. Love, which has no opposites, of which all expression are evidence
6. By giving a life-long promise, backing it up with your life for the rest of your life

Book IV, Chapter 1
Pages 72-74

1. The ability to create contexts
2. As soon as one can ask questions
3. The context "Human Being-ness"
4. Man-ness and Woman-ness

Book IV, Chapter 2
Pages 75-77

1. To assist a child to survive until the child can survive on his or her own
2. To win our Personality Contest
3. It is the place of origin of your relationship with all men and all women
4. The man and/or woman who assisted you in surviving until you could survive on your own

Book IV, Chapter 3
Pages 78-79

1. The ability to ask a question
2. Your experience of your relationship with your mother
3. It becomes your Self, that is you take a stand that it is the Absolute Truth, and you forget that you have one, that is you become your list and your list becomes you.

Book IV, Chapter 4
Pages 80-83

1. Mistake them for The Truth and become them
2. Become it and seek to prove it right
3. To not know what the stands are which you have taken about life, that is to be unconscious of them, and interpret life from them, as if they were The Truth

4. The woman contradicted your list
5. You put him or her through a rigorous behavior modification program to make your list right
6. To effect a completion, a blessing of life the way it is, and of people, the way they are

Book IV, Chapter 5
Pages 84–86

1. Before you withdrew the acknowledgment from your mother
2. To manipulate her to change and win your Personality Contest for her
3. You become inauthentic with all women
4. The restoration of the acknowledgment

Book IV, Chapter 6
Pages 87–89

1. You are the proof.
2. In your chair
3. You are returned to authenticity with all women, you grow up in relationship to your mother, and she completes motherhood
4. Inside the safe

Book IV, Chapter 7
Pages 90–93

1. In the Instinct
2. To take a stand on the absoluteness of maternal love
3. The Realm of Opposites
4. Taking the stand that love is absolute
5. In no way

Book IV, Chapter 8
Pages 94–96

1. Loss of authenticity with all women
2. Yes
3. (1) She got her job done
   (2) She loved you absolutely
4. Yours
5. Repetition
6. No.

Book V, Chapter 1
Pages 100–102

1. All
2. The Tough Guy Act

Book V, Chapter 2
Pages 103–104

1. Their ability to give birth
2. Holding the Vision

Book V, Chapter 3
Pages 105–106

1. Father
2. Survival
3. To make us happy
4. It is understandable and simple.
5. Father
6. Father
7. Father

Book V, Chapter 4
Pages 107–109

1. Around age 12–15
2. To take arbitrary stands about what one is good for in life
3. Father
4. Become exactly like someone, for example Father

Book V, Chapter 5
Pages 110–111

1. Something about being dangerous
2. The part you refuse to bless

Book V, Chapter 6
Pages 112–114

1. The Survival Plan of a child
2. You are living.
3. That he should win your Personality Contest

4. Yes.
5. Never.
6. To manipulate him to change and win your Personality Contest
7. (1) He participated in creating you
   (2) He put up with you
   (3) He loved you absolutely

Book V, Chapter 7
Pages 115–117

1. Being in an authentic, truthful relationship
2. By taking the stand that an individual's love is absolute
3. No.
4. As in a prayer

Book VI, Chapter I
Pages 121–122

1. An act of God
2. Anything
3. There Is No Answer

Book VI, Chapter 2
Pages 124–126

1. (1) Change is possible, without too much trouble, and
   (2) Happiness is a function of change.
2. Complex rats
3. Being simple, rats will eventually re-program themselves when something is not working. Humans are too complex for that.
4. The experience of satisfaction.

Book VI, Chapter 3
Pages 127–129

1. You
2. Change
3. The features you refused to bless in others
4. Nothing
5. Mother and Father, and a few others in early childhood, primarily in relationship to the parent of the same sex
6. You become a pretense.
7. There is no way.

Book VI, Chapter 4
Pages 130–131

1. A heart-felt, frequent laugh at the joke that is life, and the punch line of the joke: your own life

Book VII, Chapter 1
Pages 135–137

1. One way is economically
2. The Club
3. All men
4. Someone who has taken the stand "I am better, faster, stronger, smarter"

Book VII, Chapter 2
Pages 138–140

1. The Auxiliary
2. Any act of revenge a woman takes on a man, just for being a man and being a member of The Club
3. Nice
4. When a woman trusts a man not to leave
5. Modulate the Mean
6. Turn up the Mean and keep it turned up
7. Evidence of not being loved

Book VII, Chapter 3
Pages 141–143

1. Superior physical strength
2. That men are smarter
3. That men are faking stupidity to avoid responsibility for their actions

Book VII, Chapter 4
Pages 144–146

1. Believe them
2. Age two or three
3. Yes. Go to a well-made fairy tale for adults (a movie).

Book VII, Chapter 5
Pages 147–149

1. We are living it from the wrong fairy tales.
2. When Hell freezes over

Book VII, Chapter 6
Pages 150–151

1. They believe their fairy tales will come true.
2. A nice, non-macho, non-jerk, handsome prince

Book VIII, Chapter 1
Pages 155–158

1. One inch
2. 250,000
3. Five million years

Book VIII, Chapter 2
Pages 159–161

1. (1) Hunting
   (2) Scavenging
   (3) Gathering
   (4) Cannibalizing
2. Women
3. Made him temporarily unemployed
4. Around 15,000 years ago
5. 1/333
6. 4,000 B. C.

Book VIII, Chapter 3
Pages 162–163

1. The invention of work-saving devices
2. Agriculture and the fact that a relative few could handle food production
3. To avoid as much work as possible
4. Spare time and the trade of food and work-saving devices

Book VIII, Chapter 4
Pages 164–166

1. Each other
2. Bullying
3. Helping others
4. Compassion
5. Plasticity

Book VIII, Chapter 5
Pages 167–169

1. Love and need
2. Mean
3. Safety of the family
4. Nice
5. The dominating kind
6. Nothing

Book VIII, Chapter 6
Pages 170–172

1. The ability to develop sudden, even violent, strength
2. Resentful
3. Keep her man and give expression to her resentment
4. No way
5. Scapegoat

Book VIII, Chapter 7
Pages 173–175

1. Ownership
2. Everyone
3. Another galaxy
4. Finding your wife in bed with another man

Book VIII, Chapter 8
Pages 176–177

1. Fear of death
2. More
3. She is smarter
4. Make her jealous
5. A nice woman

Book IX, Chapter 1
Pages 181–183

1. The Being
2. The experience of existing in the Being of another
3. The temporary nature of the Self
4. We identify our sex as an important part of the Self
5. Childhood

Book IX, Chapter 2
Pages 184–185

1. Remember them like a computer and use them as weapons
2. All your life
3. To forgive all men
4. You do, and so do all the men in your life
5. Their superior intelligence

Book IX, Chapter 3
Pages 186–188

1. Surrender to the intelligence and the mean.
2. To create the man to create his experience of her way as his own
3. Respond
4. Sex and production
5. Absolute love
6. No need, you already did

Book X, Chapter 1
Pages 192–196

1. (1) Nice
   (2) Good looking
   (3) They love us
2. A Position on the Wheel of Relationship
3. One
4. Consult the evidence.
   No.
   Your Mind tells you a lie to make you look good to yourself.
5. Only you can answer this one.
6. Yes, and extremely difficult, involving much suffering

Book X, Chapter 2
Pages 197–198

1. (1) Make a list,
   (2) Name a date and time,
   (3) Create experience of having and not having the person at that date and time,
   (4) Disappear the game.
2. You are
3. When you shift your point of view from that you are lucky to have a person to that he or she is lucky to have you.

Book X, Chapter 3
Pages 199–201

1. The woman's pleasure
2. The woman's job to train the man
3. Baring physical illness or injury, no.
4. Telling the truth
5. Women lie to men about sex.
6. They all know how fragile is a man's ego.
7. Alternating acknowledgment with instruction
8. Realize how dumb he is and how much he needs training
9. The woman
10. The woman

Book X, Chapter 4
Pages 202–204

1. The woman chooses the man.
2. That the man chooses the woman
3. To protect the man's ego
4. Tolerability and recognition of her authority
5. Put himself in front of her and wait
6. Macho Male Ego
7. Be tolerable to his woman and recognize her authority
8. Recognition that next to a woman, he knows nothing about man/woman
9. Intolerability

Book X, Chapter 5
Pages 205–207

1. The form changes
2. An end
3. Bless it or curse it
4. The Condition of Failure
5. Both are interpretations
6. It isn't complete and it is not the time to "end" the relationship.

INDEX
OF WORDS, TERMS, AND PHRASES

A

Absolute
—Joy 58
—Love 187
—Love—Mother for Child.................................. 90
—Love—Father for Child................................. 101
Acceleration 15
Acknowledgment of Father 115–116
—If No Longer Living 116
Acknowledgment of Mother 84–96
—Components of 91
—If No Longer Living 93–94
—Withdrawal of 83–84
Agriculture... 159–160
Ancestry... 155–157
Anger 127
Answer—The 121–122
Aphrodisiac.. 199
Appropriateness 51
Authenticity... 51
—with Men 112–113
Autistic 72
Auxiliary—The 138–139

B

Being 9, 58, 181–182
—Purpose of in Relationship to Others 82
Being Chosen 202–203
Being Honest... 46
Boy/Girl Game 199
Bullying 164
Bus of Life.. 29–30, 167

C

Calling 186
Calling Card 135
Cannibalism... 159
Chair-ness 65–66
Change 119
Changing Relationship Forms 205
Choosing a Partner 192–193
—Who Chooses Who 202–203
Cities... 162–163
Club—The 135–136, 167, 168, 184

Commerce 162–163
Compassion 51, 168, 179, 181–187
Condition
  —of Failure 205
  —of Life 205
Context of Absolute Love 65
Context of Entertainment 13
Contexts 65
Create a Relationship Game 197
Creating Relationship 190

D

Dead Relationship 205
Dishonesty 45
Doing Honest 45–56
Domination 135–136, 168
Driver's Seat of the Bus of Life 30

E

End—The 29
Ending Relationship 190, 205–206
Enlightened Man Act 168
Enlightenment
  —Real 130
Ex-Husbands 206
Ex-Wives 206

F

Failure 205
Fairy Tales 144–145
Family
  —as a Position on the Wheel of Relationship 194
  —Purpose of 105
Father 98
  —Definition of 76
  —Purpose of 112
  —Role 170
Fear of Men 36–37
  —from Experience of Father 110
Female Intelligence 150
Feminine Principle 36–37
Feminization of Poverty 135
Fetus Envy 103
Firewood-ness 66
Five Million Years 155–156
Forgiving
  —a Man 184
  —a Woman 186

Functional Intelligence 51
Future 28–30

G

Game of Life 130
Garden of Eden 58
Gathering 159
Good and Bad 52
Good Times—as a Position on the Wheel of Relationship 194
Good-looking 192
Grand Cosmic Game 128
Gurus 130

H

Hand-to-Mouth Existence 30, 159
Heaven 62
Hell 62
Higher Purpose—as a Position on the Wheel of Relationship 194
Home-maker 164
Homemaking 164–165
Honesty 42, 44–46
   —an Adult Definition 45
   —a Child's Definition 45
Hunting 164–165
Hunting Instinct 164

I

Inauthenticity—with Women 85
Individual's Relationship to the Whole 39–40
Insane Jealousy 173
Internal Critic 127
Intolerability in a Man 203
Inventor—Man as 162

J

Jealousy
   —Female 176
   —Male 173–174
Jerks 203
Journey of Humankind Through Time 155–157
Justifiable Homicide 173

K

Kingdom of Heaven 62

L

Leaving Patterns 13
Lesson of Relationship 205
List
  —Men 110–111
  —Women 78–82
Living Happily Ever After 147
Longevity—as a Position on the Wheel of Relationship 194
Looking Good—as a Position on the Wheel of Relationship 194
Love
  —and Communication—as a Position on the Wheel of Relationship 194
  —and Need 167–168
  —as a Sacred Promise 208
  —the Abundance of 192
Loyalty 208

M

Macho Male Ego 32–34, 100
Maintaining Relationship 190
Make a Difference 39–40
Male Stupidity 141–142
Man 135
Man Acts 202
Man-ness 73
Man/Woman Game 199
Man/Woman Relationship 21–23
Mating Procedure 202–203
Matrix 39–40
Mean 138–139, 167, 170–171, 176, 187
  —Origins 170–171
  —and the Woman's authority 203
Mind 10, 15, 82
Miracles 11
Money—as a Position on the Wheel of Relationship 194
Mother 70, 72–94
  —Definition of 75
Murder 173
Mutual Assured Destruction 32–34
Mutual Support—as a Position on the Wheel of Relationship..... 194
My Pleasure—as a Position on the Wheel of Relationship 193

N

Near-death 1
Nice 139, 167, 192
  —Virgin Princess.................................... 147–148
  —Woman 176
Non-Macho Prince 150–151
Nuclear Weapons 29

P

PWR 192–195
Paradise 58, 61
Parents—Purpose of 75
Patterns 124–125
Personality 127, 181
  —Change 91
  —Contest 75
  —Contest—for Mother 84
Plasticity 165
Position on Wheel of Relationship 192–195
Potential for Violence 141
Presence of God 1
Pretense of Enlightenment 130
Price for Dishonesty 52–53
Price for Domination 138–139
Producing 186
Purpose 181
Purpose of a Parent 75–76

R

Reality—The 56
Realm of Absolutes 49, 61–62
Realm of Opposites 15, 56, 59
  —In One's Experience of Mother 90
  —Method to Get Out of 61–62
Reconstructing Reality 65–66
Recreating Relationship With Mother 90
Responding 186
Results of Honesty 51–53
Road of History 29–30

S

Sacred Promise 208
Sainthood 113
Scapegoat 105–106
Scavenger—Human as 159
Self 181
  —Creation of as Opposite of Father 107–108
  —Definition 9
  —in Relationship to Women 80
Sex 186, 199–200
  —as a Position on the Wheel of Relationship 194
Sin 48–49
Source
  —of Human Intelligence 72
  —of a Man's Pleasure in Sex 106
Stakes of The Man/Woman Game 25–26, 28–30

Success 51, 205
—as a Position on the Wheel of Relationship 194
Surrender 127–128
Survival Plan (of a child) 112
System that Excludes its Creator 87–88

T

Teaching a Man About Sex 199–200
Technology 162–163, 170
Tolerability in a Man 202–203
Tough
—Guy Act 98, 100, 103, 108
—Love 112
Trainability in a Man Regarding Sex 200
Tree of Right and Wrong 58
Truth—The 48–49

U

Upset 7, 15
—in Relationship 206

V

Violence—the Potential For 141–142
Vision 103–104

W

Wheel of Relationship 192–195
Withdrawal of Mother's Acknowledgment 84–85
Woman 138
Woman's Authority 202–203
Woman Power 199–200, 203
Woman-ness 73
World—The 58

Y

Your Pleasure—as a Position on the Wheel of Relationship 194